Just Gone

Just Gone

Just Gone

True Stories of Persecution
for Love and Life

Jo DeLuzio

RE:BOOKS

Copyright © Jo DeLuzio.

All rights reserved.

www.rebooks.ca

Published in Canada by RE:BOOKS.

ADDRESS:
RE:BOOKS
Brookfield Place
181 Bay Street
Suite 1800
Toronto, Ontario
M5J 2T9
Canada

www.rebooks.ca

First RE:BOOKS Edition: October 2024

ISBN: 978-1-998206-02-5
eBook ISBN: 978-1-998206-03-2

Printed and bound in Canada.

1 3 5 7 9 10 8 6 4 2

Cover Design By: Chloe Faith Robinson

THEIR STORIES

AUTHOR'S NOTE

This book contains descriptions of physical and sexual violence, including instances of torture and rape, which regrettably reflect the real experiences of people whose stories are being told. Reader discretion is advised.

Dedication

To 2SLGBTQ+ refugees everywhere, whose journeys speak to the incredible resilience of the human spirit. I am humbled by your courage.

Introduction

World Pride, an event that began in Rome, Italy in 2000, now occurs in different cities around the world every two or three years. When Toronto, Canada was the host in June of 2014, I attended the affiliated human rights conference, which focused on several issues such as trans rights and activism, approaches to HIV/AIDS, empowering youth, and 2SLGBTQ+ refugees. The conference provided opportunities for people from around the world to share their stories and have conversations about global issues impacting these communities. I attended the conference because, as a queer-identified woman, I wanted to do something more meaningful than watch a parade during Pride month. As well, one of my adult children who identifies as a person who is trans, nonbinary, and asexual was sitting on a discussion panel, and I wanted to give them my support. Quite unexpectedly, this conference had a profound impact on my life.

Even though I am reasonably well-informed, I had no true understanding of the magnitude of the egregious human rights violations occurring against 2SLGBTQ+ people globally. Nor did I have any clue about the process of seeking asylum in another country for people with non-conventional sexual orientations, gender identity, or gender expression, and the tremendous barriers they might encounter along their way.

On the second day of the conference, I walked to lunch with a young man from a small African nation that I happened to sit beside at one of the morning sessions. He spoke openly and honestly about the abuse he has endured as a gay man. He explained that every day when he left home, he had to consciously think about where and *how* he would walk. In his town, the way he moves had been deemed too feminine to be acceptable for a man. Reactions he had received to his gait ranged from name-calling and verbal assaults to brutal beatings. He stated this information in a matter-of-fact way, like it was nothing out of the ordinary, just a routine occurrence. Because it was.

This short conversation left an indelible mark on my brain. I couldn't wrap my head around it. I am a person of significant privilege, and when I walk out my door in the morning, I go where I please. It never crosses my mind that the way I move might offend someone or put my life in danger.

My home is Toronto, Canada. For the most part, people who identify as 2SLGBTQ+ are viewed as part of the general makeup of individuals who reside here. Marriage for gay people, which had already been occurring in most Canadian provinces and one territory as far back as 2003, became legalized across the entire country in 2005. Discrimination based on sexual orientation and gender identity or expression is against the law, as is hate speech. On paper, 2SLGBTQ+ people in Canada enjoy the same legal rights with respect to housing and employment as everyone else. They also have the same access to adoption, surrogacy, and in vitro fertilization (IVF) treatments as heteronormative, gender-conforming people. For Canadians, especially for those who reside in some of the larger cities such as Vancouver, Montreal, or Toronto, it can be very easy to be lulled into believing that rainbow flags are welcome everywhere. As a queer woman, I remain cautious.

But this conversation isn't really about flags. It is about human rights and freedoms. Although the number of countries legalizing gay marriage has increased to thirty-five (out of about 195 countries in the world),[1] there are still approximately seventy-one countries that outlaw gay sex. Reports vary, but in twelve of these countries, homosexual acts are punishable by death. As well, there are around fourteen countries that criminalize "cross-dressing" or wearing clothing that appears to be designed for the "opposite" gender.

These examples are just the tip of the proverbial iceberg. Around the world, there are numerous countries where 2SLGBTQ+ people are denied access to housing, education, health care, and employment. In some areas, people with non-conventional sexual orientations and gender identities or expressions are viewed as lower than animals, not worthy of life. The violence and hate directed against them seems almost impossible to endure. In immeasurable cases, they are being bullied, ridiculed, sexually assaulted, beaten, tortured, and even hunted down and then literally slaughtered. When they hide who they are for their own protection, they live in constant fear of being outed, of being thrown out onto the streets like garbage, of losing their families and possibly having their children taken away. In many places, the laws do little, if anything, to offer protection. Sometimes, it is the law makers and enforcers who are participating in and encouraging the brutalization.

To be clear, this isn't *only* about respecting the use of pronouns, of being appalled that books with any hint of queer characters are being banned, or of resolving arguments over where we think people should pee. There is not a "gay agenda," and 2SLGBTQ+ people do not believe that their rights trump anyone else's. Quite simply, gay and transgender rights are human rights. And make no mistake, hateful and discriminatory acts against people who identify as belonging to any 2SLGBTQ+ community have been gaining momentum and are on the rise globally.

During lunch that day at the conference, I naïvely asked this young man why he didn't remain in Toronto and apply for refugee status. It was a logical question. Or so I thought. It seemed like such a simple solution.

His answer still haunts me. He said remaining in Canada was not an option. He had to return home to continue the fight for the rights of all 2SLGBTQ+ people in his country, even though he knew his activism would most likely result in his death. The courage of his convictions was astounding. I was embarrassed I had ever posed this question. I often wonder if this man is still alive today. It seems unlikely.

After we parted ways, my brain spun around like an overwound top with a myriad of questions. What happens to the people who are 2SLGBTQ+ in his country, or any other country, who fear for their lives and don't want to stay? Where would they go for help? Is there help? How do they know where to go? Would the authorities in these countries even permit people to leave? Or must they flee secretly, disappear from their previous life, and be gone? How does a 2SLGBTQ+ person become a refugee? Is the process difficult?

What does it really mean to be a refugee who is 2SLGBTQ+?

Before attempting to answer any of these questions, it is important to note that in 2024, the world is in a humanitarian crisis with conservative estimates of over 30 million refugees who have fled their home countries, and over 100 million people who have been internally displaced.[2] Millions of people worldwide are food and shelter compromised, with no relief in sight. There are countries where innocent people, including children, are the causalities, and sometimes the targets of war. Worldwide, people are trying to escape persecution for religious, ethnic, and political reasons. Many countries are guilty of executing horrific human rights violations, making them unsafe.

2SLGBTQ+ people face all the same hardships and challenges as anyone else. They exist everywhere in the world, including in countries ravaged by earthquakes, hurricanes, tsunamis, fires, floods, and any other natural disaster. They too can be persecuted because of their ethnicity, religion, political alliance, or where they are geographically located. However, in many nations, they fight an additional battle—one against their personhood. There are areas of the world that strive to cleanse themselves of any 2SLGBTQ+ people, to annihilate them, as if their very presence is a threat to humankind.

And when they cannot endure their existence any longer, and they need to run, where are they supposed to go?

The unfortunate reality that is pervasive for 2SLGBTQ+ people seeking asylum is that the brutal persecution they face isn't the only thing threatening their lives. It's existing in a state of destitution on the fringes of society that eventually kills them. As well, in a multitude of countries, suicide is the leading cause of death among youth who identify as being 2SLGBTQ+, and many of them attempt suicide before the age of twenty-five.[3] These numbers are staggering, especially when you consider that many young people who take their own lives may be closeted. Therefore, their deaths would not be recorded as being associated with their sexual orientation or gender identity.

My primary motivation for writing this book was to increase awareness and provide education about how those who are 2SLGBTQ+ are treated and oppressed globally. No matter how the situation is analyzed, the sheer amount of violence targeting people with non-conventional sexual orientations and gender identities or expressions is overwhelming, and there doesn't seem to be much public outcry. Information about what is happening to people who are 2SLGBTQ+ seldom makes the news and it doesn't appear to be on the radar of very many people. I believe this book is one small step forward in bringing attention to this human rights crisis.

As difficult as it might have been for the people that I interviewed to share their stories and relive their experiences, they wanted them told. Their journeys speak to the incredible resilience of the human spirit, the unfathomable power of the desire to live a truthful and authentic life, and the unflagging fight of marginalized and oppressed people to demand rights and to occupy space, no matter the cost. Those who have somehow managed to escape and land in Canada as refugees have the right to be protected and feel safe, and for that to happen, they need to be seen. They are entitled to live their true lives. Their stories provide first-hand accounts about what is occurring to people who have non-conventional sexual orientations, gender identities, or gender expressions in their home countries. They put real faces to the statistics that might occasionally be reported in the news.

Despite all the odds stacked against them, some people do manage to escape one country and enter another as refugees because of their 2SLGBTQ+ status. However, the few stories I have seen in the media describing these journeys have been brief and largely focused on homosexual men. My own writing reflects this demographic. I did have the opportunity to meet two women in Toronto who overcame seemingly insurmountable barriers and entered Canada as refugees because their lives were in danger as lesbian women in their home countries. However, they continue to fear for their safety, and did not want their stories told in this book. They did agree to answer my questions and we spent several hours talking. Their insights into the reality of 2SLGBTQ+ women internationally have been invaluable to me, and I hope are reflected in my writing. I am grateful they agreed to speak with me. But in the end, I was only able to share the story of one cisgender woman in this book. Why is this?

The exact reasons are quite likely numerous and complex, and I can only speculate.

Could it be that the oppression of women as well as the pervasive existence of gender-based violence worldwide makes fleeing their home countries difficult, if not impossible?

Numerous countries are patriarchal, and women are subjugated socially, educationally, economically, and legally. They are not permitted to be away from their family unless they are married, and then they become the responsibility, and sometimes the property, of their husbands. Finding and creating safe meeting places is impossible if you are forbidden to leave your house, or when you are continually being watched. Poverty or economic destitution without the support of a man are absolutely conditions that might keep gay women closeted.

2SLGBTQ+ women existing in countries where they have no rights, reproductive or otherwise, and endure domestic violence, rape, insufficient health care, and denial of education or any autonomy, will likely never have the chance to live their true sexual orientation or gender identity. Their fight is for survival and the survival of their children.

Countries that are the most oppressive to women are often the poorest, making survival for anyone challenging. Although it is difficult to get exact numbers, there appear to be at least thirty countries that continue to practice female genital mutilation.[4] These girls usually haven't experienced puberty and are under the age of eight, sometimes they're even babies. Such procedures leave women with serious physical health issues such as paralysis of the bladder, incontinence, painful urination, menstruation, and sexual intercourse, and difficulty during childbirth. They also suffer from mental health issues because of this dismemberment. According to the World Health Organization, about 200 million girls and women worldwide are affected by having their genitals mutilated in some form.[4] 2SLGBTQ+ women, or any woman living under these conditions, have little, if any, hope of choosing how and where they might like to live, and with whom.

Even in countries where women are allowed an education and have some human rights, social control is much stronger than it is for men. In some places, unmarried women cannot hold passports and are not granted travel visas. They are certainly not going to find the support they need to seek refugee status elsewhere.

In many cultures, while gay men are viewed as deviant, lesbian women are presumed to have not met the "right" man. In countries such as South Africa, India, Zimbabwe, and Jamaica, "correctional rape" can occur to treat and cure same-sex desires in women. Although this likely wouldn't be considered a hate crime in these countries, that is precisely what this heinous act amounts to. It is homophobic, cruel, and baseless.

Heteronormative sex tends to focus on the penis, and sexual acts not involving a penis penetrating a vagina are not always viewed as "real" sex. Sex between two women does not require a penis and doesn't have to involve a vagina. Therefore, sexual acts between two women are judged by many cultures as not constituting real sex.

The pressure to marry is still very high around the world, including with many families in North America. Arranged marriages are common practice in some cultures. Women who are forced into marriage through family arrangement or societal expectation have little chance to escape. It would be particularly challenging when there are young children involved.

When considering the position of women within this global context, it is not surprising that we do not hear many stories of women who leave their country as refugees because of their identity as someone who is 2SLGBTQ+. It must be incomprehensibly difficult for them to do so.

But we must ask ourselves, what kind of world is it for 2SLGBTQ+ women, when they must continue to hide and live in fear?

The world is organized into binaries, where there are males and females, both with prescribed and expected roles to fulfill. Traditionally, masculinity was revered while femininity (as well as feminine traits) was ridiculed and devalued. Historically, men were expected to dominate politically, economically, and socially. Sexually, men were expected to conquer women, often as many women as possible, while women were supposed to remain chaste, and submissive. Although things have been slowly changing, this perspective is persistent and continues to be reflected in politics as well as in the media.

It should come as no surprise that a world that values men and the traits associated with masculinity would oppress women, and diminish anything conventionally associated with being female. This might explain why masculine-looking and masculine-acting gay men can sometimes escape brutality in aggressively homophobic countries. They are not visible because they do not adhere to the stereotype that gay men, who are perceived to be weak and inferior, walk and talk like women (also viewed as weak and inferior.) As well, they are assumed to be the "penetrator" in a homosexual relationship, the role that a male is supposed to fulfill. There is no question that feminine-presenting men are more likely to be the targets of homophobic violence, regardless of their sexual orientation or gender identity.[5]

Femmephobia spills over into the appalling treatment of transgender people, where much of the violence and hate is directed at transgender women. Data from around the world indicates that transwomen and trans feminine people are at high risk of being sexually assaulted, raped, beaten, and murdered. People who are transgender who identify as being Black, brown, or Indigenous are especially vulnerable.[6]

Although gender and sexuality are two different things, homosexual men might be viewed as a threat to mandatory heteronormativity because they may not be perceived as being masculine enough, and they are not sexually dominating women. This could be one reason why a host of different countries hold the view that men engaging in sex with each other is a horrible offense, while sexual acts between two women are not that terrible.

For instance, under Islamic criminal law in Iran, homosexual acts between men, even if consensual, can be punishable by death, whereas sex acts between women usually result in lashings. Similarly, the law in Mauritania stipulates that the punishment for homosexual acts between men is death, but sex acts between women are reportedly punishable by only a small fine along with a short prison term. Along these same lines, the criminal codes of some countries, such as Turkmenistan, take things one step further. They render homosexual acts between men as illegal, with a variety of punishments including years of incarceration, huge fines, beatings, or death. However, sex acts between women are not even mentioned. The real crime appears to be that the men are not fulfilling the expectations of their gender role. And perhaps, women are not deemed important enough to be prosecuted.

Anti-sodomy laws around the world might place gay men at greater risk of persecution than others with different sexual orientations. From a religious perspective, sodomy is specifically named as aberrant in the Old Testament, the Koran, and the Torah, and is therefore considered sinful in Christianity, Islam, and Judaism respectively. Although people of different sexual orientations and gender identities willingly participate in anal sex, it is more stereotypically associated with gay men.

Most countries do not have laws explicitly safeguarding people who are transgender, and in many countries, people who are transgender or gender diverse can be prevented from securing employment and housing. As well, they can be arrested on bogus charges such as debauchery (e.g., Egypt), impersonating the opposite sex (e.g., Kuwait, Nigeria, Abu Dhabi, Dubai, Malaysia), and lewd behaviour (e.g., Morocco). In some areas of the world, transgender people are arrested and charged with prostitution, when they are not prostitutes (e.g., Azerbaijan, Egypt, Indonesia). In other words, their very existence is seen as a crime. Countries such as Saudi Arabia, North Korea, and Sudan forbid people from dressing in clothing considered to be for the "opposite" gender and do not permit men to wear makeup. Consequently, drag queens must perform underground in many areas of the world to avoid being arrested.

Before you try to convince yourself that these things only happen "somewhere else," let's be clear, Western society is not guilt-free. In the United States, where sexual activity between consenting, same-sex adults is legal, and hate crimes because of sexual orientation or gender identity are punishable according to federal laws, there were over 250 anti-2SLGBTQ+ bills introduced in 2021.[7] Even though most were unsuccessful, twenty-four were enacted on.[7]

In 2022, attacks on people who are transgender, especially children, have continued to grow in the United States. According to the most recent Human Rights Watch World Report,[8] which is from 2023, more than 150 bills have been introduced in the United States with the purpose of removing rights and access to specialized health care for people who are transgender. Ten states passed laws stating children had to play sports consistent with their biological sex, not their gender identity; and at least six states have mandated that children use the bathroom at school consistent with their biological sex, not their gender identity. In the last year, over a dozen bathroom bills have been filed in fifteen states. What am I missing? When I go into a public women's washroom, there are individual stalls. I don't see anyone's genitals, not even my own.

Both Arizona and Alabama have passed legislation to ban gender-affirming care for children and youth, and several states exclude medical coverage of these services in their Medicaid. Some states are in the process of attempting to pass laws that would not only forbid gender-confirming care for minors but would also require transgender youth to detransition. Across the United States, healthcare workers who choose to provide gender-confirming treatment and care report they are often harassed and encounter violent attacks.

On another front, an appalling twenty states introduced "don't say gay or trans" bills,[9] which would have restricted any discussion of sexuality or gender identity in the schools, although Florida and Alabama were the only states successful in enacting their legislation. Florida is one state where numerous and blatant attempts to erase us, and any mention of us, from the school system continue in full force. And the list goes on.

Let's not be naïve about this. Not all incidents of homophobia and transphobia are blatant. Attempts to roll back the laws protecting the rights of 2SLGBTQ+ people are sometimes masked or disguised as something else, such as protection of freedom of religion, or ensuring safety of children; both laudable causes, but neither of which have anything to do with people who are 2SLGBTQ+.

Even in Canada, a country that has taken many strides forward and prides itself with acceptance and welcoming of all people, there are still issues. Statistics Canada has documented that police-reported hate crimes because of sexual identity have been increasing since 2018.[10] The actual numbers are not high, but they are there, and they used to be closer to zero. During 2023, members of the

2SLGBTQ+ communities and their advocates have reported an increase in threats and hate crimes because of sexual orientation, gender identity and expression, and even against drag queens. It is important to point out that these numbers capture only those incidents reported to police and are then considered a hate crime after an investigation. Many 2SLGBTQ+ people in Canada, and elsewhere in the world, do not report hate crimes directed at them because they feel humiliated, they are afraid of retribution, and they may believe that they won't be taken seriously by the police when filing their report.

While available, wait times in some areas of Canada for people seeking gender-confirming surgeries can be long, and other medical treatments for people who are transgender are not necessarily easily accessible or covered by provincial health insurance. Medical and healthcare practitioners can be uneducated on the needs of people who are 2SLGBTQ+, and as such, more training is required around providing appropriate and non-oppressive services to these communities.

All things considered; Canada continues to be one of the desired destinations for many 2SLGBTQ+ refugees. Immigration, Refugees and Citizenship Canada (IRCC) actively supports the sponsorship of refugees who face persecution because of their sexual orientation, gender identity or expression, or their HIV status. IRCC also offers information, resources, and system navigation, as well as links to other ally organizations, in addition to providing financial support for the Rainbow Refugee Society. The Blended Visa Office-Refereed Program (BVOR) matches refugees identified by the United Nations High Commissioner for Refugees (UNHCR) with private sponsors in Canada. It is important to note that UNHCR Canada does not intervene or influence the process of deciding who will be considered a refugee in Canada, and whether a refugee can be resettled to Canada.

The Supreme Court of Canada accepts sexual orientation as a group that qualifies for refugee status for possible admission into Canada. As of October of 2023, the Immigration and Refugee Board of Canada *Chairperson's Guideline 4: Gender Considerations in Proceedings Before the Immigration and Refugee Board* was amended. Under *Section 2. Application*, section 2.2 now reads:

> The focus of the 1996 Guideline was on women refugee claimants. This Guideline broadens the focus to include all genders and gender identities, while recognizing that women and girls and SOGIESC (sexual orientation, gender identity and expression and sex characteristics) individuals are disproportionately impacted by gender-based violence, gender inequality and discrimination, all of which are human rights issues.[11]

Although the guidelines address avoiding myths, stereotypes, and incorrect assumptions, proving refugee status can still be complex. It can be challenging for someone to prove their 2SLGBTQ+ status, especially if their behaviour is adjudicated using a Westernized, heteronormative, gender-binary lens. So, yes, we are moving forward. But progress is slow, and it is not linear.

The journey to Canada, or any country deemed safe for people who are being persecuted because of their sexual or gender identity, is not a cakewalk. It requires financial resources to flee one's country, and people need to have access to accurate information before they can do so. Such information might be censored in their country, and even if it isn't, one cannot access anything if they are surviving minute by minute on the streets.

Even when someone identifies a possible escape route, people who have lived a deeply closeted existence for survival will not have photos, texts, and emails proving that they have a non-conventional sexual orientation or gender identity. How do you prove you are gay if you have never existed as an out gay person? How do you have "technological" proof, when you exist in poverty, and have no access to technology? Understandably, when refugees are from countries where police and other authorities have contributed to their abuses, they may be afraid to be open and honest about their identity with staff from the UNHCR or Immigration and Refugee Board (IRB) workers. Realistically, how can they know who to trust and who will offer them protection?

Culture and language can present barriers to becoming accepted as a 2SLGBTQ+ refugee, and differing terminology and vocabulary can be confusing. For example, there is not a word for "lesbian" in my wife's native African language, and some languages do not have an equivalent word for "transgender."

The list of potential barriers is exhausting.

After meeting with people who came to Canada because of their sexual orientation or gender identity and learning of their stories first-hand, I recognize just how ridiculous my assumption was that seeking refugee status because of 2SLGBTQ+ identity could ever be a simple solution. Regardless of the urgency of their situation, a person who is 2SLGBTQ+ can't just waltz into another country, be welcomed with open arms, and get handed a new life.

Settling into a different country and culture can be extremely difficult, and the pain of a person's previous life is not suddenly erased just because they are physically located in a different place. Moreover, many of these people continue to battle post-traumatic stress disorder (PTSD), and sometimes they encounter hate and discrimination even in supposedly safe countries.

Once people arrive in Canada, and it has been decided they have a right to submit a claim, their case is referred to the IRB. Upon entry into the country, they require immediate housing, and numerous other supports. People cannot realistically settle into a productive new life while they are awaiting their case to go before the IRB, and in 2023 the wait time was reportedly approximately twenty-four months. While Canada has demonstrated a commitment to resettling a significant number of refugees, especially those who are most vulnerable, this wait time is considered by many to be too long, and the government itself has identified that more work needs to be done in creating opportunities and exploring possible educational paths in addition to providing safe housing assistance.

In writing this book, I have had the privilege of meeting people who sought asylum in Canada because of their 2SLGBTQ+ status. This book is not just full of their stories. It is filled with their dreams for the future. I often wonder: every time someone with a non-conventional sexual orientation, gender identity, or gender expression gets murdered anywhere in the world, do we all become accessories to that murder because we have failed to do anything to prevent it?

Perhaps offering asylum for people who are being persecuted because of their 2SLGBTQ+ identity is akin to reducing a life sentence. It is like sparing someone from the death penalty when they have committed no crime. They can finally be liberated from the chains of the atrocities they have endured. It is their inalienable right to be treated with respect and kindness, and to enjoy the same human rights as people with a conventional sexual orientation or gender identity or expression.

It is one of my greatest hopes that after you have read this book and met these courageous young people through the words on these pages, you will be asking yourself how many more 2SLGBTQ+ people need to die before the world stands up and takes notice.

Sherwin:
Land of Wood and Water

I first met Sherwin at the 2014 Human Rights Conference when Toronto hosted World Pride. June was sweltering hot that year, and I sat on the ground under a magnificent tree in a vain attempt to secure some shade. Sherwin noticed me sitting there and plunked himself right down beside me. His opener was that we had attended the same session with the incredible human rights activist Cleve Jones. Jones served as a student intern with the great Harvey Milk, and he first originated the idea of the AIDS Memorial Quilt, which now has well over 100,000 names, and has raised over three million dollars for organizations serving people with HIV/AIDS. I didn't recognize Sherwin from the session, because in true Jo fashion, I had been sitting in the front row.

Sherwin is a talker. And so am I. We chatted about what a thrill it was to meet Cleve Jones, World Pride, the conference, and the weather. We quickly learned that we both identified as queer, and that he had come to Toronto as a refugee because he feared for his life in his home country of Jamaica. He commented that I didn't look gay, but I suppose he didn't look much like how I imagined an ex-refugee to appear either.

Suddenly, all the questions that had been ricocheting around my brain since I had met the young man from Africa whose life was in danger by his manner of walking, came spilling out of my mouth. I couldn't stop myself. What were the circumstances that made him leave? What was his journey like? How did he successfully transition into life here given all the cultural differences he encountered? How did it feel to completely uproot himself from his family and his country? To effectively disappear?

Sherwin laughed his incredible laugh and deflected most of my questions. He didn't share much with me about his personal journey as a refugee from Jamaica. Mostly he spoke about how fortunate he felt that he had significant financial support to enable him to escape. He was clear that 2SLGBTQ+ people in his country who are marginalized and living in poverty have little, if any, hope of ever leaving. Or even of staying alive. Our conversation quickly morphed into a discussion about 2SLGBTQ+ refugees.

Since 2014, Sherwin and I maintained sporadic contact. Needless to say, he was the first person I contacted when I decided to write this book and he was more than willing to have his story told. He also contacted other people he knew who had come to Toronto as refugees more recently and asked them if they would be willing to meet with me to describe their journeys.

I met with Sherwin on three different occasions to secure a detailed account of his journey. For the first interview, we meet in a coffee shop in the Church-Wellesley Village, a 2SLGBTQ+ focused neighbourhood in Toronto, Canada. Since he was not a stranger, there was not any of that awkwardness that can happen at first meetings. We chatted about nothing for a few minutes.

Conversation flowed freely, and it felt like I was sitting under a tree, shooting the breeze with an old friend.

Sherwin began his interview by telling me a story. In June of 2004, Brian Williamson, the most well-known gay rights activist in Jamaica, was repeatedly stabbed in his home in Kingston.[12] Police reported that the motive for the killing was a robbery, which might be true, but the death certainly looked like a hate crime. Everyone, including any 2SLGBTQ+ or human rights activists, was convinced that Brian was killed because of his sexual orientation. Regardless, after hearing about this death, the public reacted quickly. People gathered in the streets to celebrate his death, chanting *"Batty man fi dead!"* This essentially translates from the Jamaican Patois into "f*gs should die." At the time of this incident, Sherwin was nineteen years old.

After that, Sherwin realized he would have to leave his country and his family. He didn't know when and he didn't know how. But he knew he wasn't safe. If Williamson, a man wealthy enough to live in a gated community, could not escape the violence directed at homosexuals, then Sherwin believed he had little chance of surviving. Like Brian, he too is a *batty bwoy* (derogatory term in Jamaican Patois for a homosexual male).

I was embarrassed to admit to Sherwin that I had never heard of Brian Williamson or the tragic end to his life before our conversation, and I had difficulty processing his words. How full of hate did people have to be to cheer the murder of a homosexual? I was overcome with emotion, grief for a man that I never met, and the pain that came from knowing I am abhorred just for existing. Tears slowly rolled down my cheeks.

Sherwin handed me one of his napkins without commenting and continued speaking.

He was born in Mandeville, Jamaica, the second of five children, and the only male child. Sherwin has a thin build with very muscular legs, much like a professional soccer player. He's not particularly tall, about 5'8" to 5'10", with sparkling dark, brown eyes. Although Sherwin's hair is curly, his curls are not super tight, they are more like spirals or springy coils, and since I have known him, he has kept his hair on the long side, long enough to be pulled into a ponytail or scooped up into a loose bun. He is very handsome, with a bright smile that lights up his entire face.

Sherwin's family are devout followers of the Seventh-day Adventist Church. Despite the stereotypes of single-mother families in Jamaica, he did not grow up poor and fatherless. His mother was a nurse at a local hospital and his father was a musician. They were not rich, but he always had clean clothes and enough to eat. It was a happy home, full of song. Music was a huge part of his family's life growing up, not just his father's compositions, but also religious music glorifying God.

From a very early age, Sherwin felt responsible for the girls in his family. His father was often in Kingston overnight for gigs, and he expected Sherwin to be "the man" of the household from the time he was seven or eight years old. His assigned job was to keep everyone safe. Sherwin reflected upon this, understanding that it was a tremendous amount of pressure to put on a little boy. Despite it all, he maintained that his father was basically a good man who believed very strongly that men were tough and strong because God made them that way. The inarguable perspective that was conveyed to Sherwin and his sisters was that God made women to be nurturers and care for the children and home, while men had to be the protectors and the heads of the households. Women were expected to be in submission to men, even to male children.

As a child, Sherwin was small for his age, and he was not that interested in sports. The boys in his neighbourhood liked to arm wrestle or play a game that Sherwin described as resembling American football. Sherwin wasn't good at either. He never enjoyed aggressive or high contact sports activities. To this day, he still does not.

Consequently, the older boys called him *batty bwoy* and *chi chi bwoy* and ruthlessly taunted him. Sherwin didn't really know what those words meant, but he knew he didn't want to be one of whatever it was they were calling him. He was not alone in being teased. Apparently, when he was a child, all the physically weaker boys were ridiculed and called these same names. They were also called girls, and various euphemisms for female genitalia.

One day, Sherwin asked his father about batty bwoys. His father told him that these men should be beaten and urinated on, and that they deserved to die. Even though Sherwin still didn't know what made someone a batty bwoy, he got the message loud and clear that they were worthless people. His father also told him that you could always tell a *batty bwoy* because of the way they walked and talked. Sherwin remembers that he wondered whether they spoke a different language, but he was too afraid to ask any questions.

Sherwin's saving grace was that he could run fast for long distances without tiring. Running isn't combative, but it requires power and strength, and so it is an acceptable thing for a boy to do. Due to his small size, light build, and long legs, Sherwin could easily outrun the strongest arm wrestler in his peer group.

As Sherwin grew older, the pressure to be a man felt like a heavy weight on his back. By the time he was twelve or thirteen, his friends continually badgered him about when he was going to find himself a girlfriend. They thought that boys who did not have sex with a girl by the time they were thirteen or fourteen must be batty bwoys. Older boys and men, even male relatives, encouraged and even expected Sherwin to have sex with as many girls as possible. This was deemed necessary to prove his virility and his manhood.

Apparently, this attitude didn't necessarily change as the boys got older. Many of them continued to have sex with multiple girls while they had girlfriends, and they fully expected to continue this behaviour after marriage. Sherwin explained that his friends believed that men were entitled to do whatever they wanted with women. It was generally accepted that women were there for the enjoyment of men, and to take care of any resulting children. This viewpoint distresses Sherwin greatly. He could not then and cannot now stand the thought of men treating his sisters, or any women, in that way.

In Sherwin's hometown, once girls hit puberty, they were supposed to appear sexy, and their families were proud when they dressed provocatively, but they were not actually supposed to engage in sex. And since a good girl can't be prepared for intercourse, these girls were at risk of pregnancy and sexually transmitted diseases. Sherwin tried using the fear of impregnating a girl as his main excuse with his friends for not engaging in sex. However, his friends assured him that since a virgin cannot get pregnant, he just had to select a virgin for his first sexual conquest. These boys *genuinely* believed what they were saying was true.

Sherwin and his friends received no formal education on sex, birth control, or sexually transmitted diseases. Most of his peers who were sexually active were doing so without knowledge of any medical or health consequences of their actions. Sherwin personally knew several teenage boys that had fathered children with different girls. None of them assumed any responsibility for those babies.

Sherwin considers himself fortunate that his mother was a nurse and he had access to factual health information. However, he felt he could not challenge the advice of his peers, even when he knew they were wrong. The other boys already had enough to tease him about. He didn't need them calling him a nurse or teasing him for behaving like a female. Sherwin usually remained silent during the many painful discussions his friends engaged in about their sexual prowess and girls' bodies or breast sizes.

Sherwin attained most of his adult height between fourteen and fifteen years of age, and by that time, his hormones were raging. He knew he was different from the other boys, and he had figured out why. When his friends drooled over women walking on the street, his body responded only when he viewed men. While he appreciated the physical beauty of women, he was not sexually attracted to them. And he never said anything to anyone about it. He knew he couldn't. He hoped he would grow out of it.

At school, he scanned the schoolyard and wondered if there were other boys like him around. He knew enough to recognize that being small or weak didn't mean you were sexually attracted to other boys. Nor did showing emotion, although from a young age, any boys who cried were teased mercilessly and sometimes punched and kicked. Sherwin noted that the teachers never seemed to notice this when it occurred on the playground.

Sherwin and his male peers were socialized to be masculine and strong. Aggression against the more feminine or gentle boys was encouraged, and Sherwin felt it was further reinforced by people in authority such as police, teachers, and even many parents of children at his school. According to Sherwin, the common belief was that the sissy boys needed to get "the girl" beaten out of them. Boys and men should never cry. Showing emotion meant that you were weak and girly.

Sherwin explained that he referred to teenage boys raised with a macho mentality as "mega males," a term he believed he coined. (After I left our meeting, I googled mega male, and it just happens to be the name of a performance-enhancing supplement for men. I am not sure why, but when I phoned Sherwin to give him this little tidbit of information, we both laughed uncontrollably for several minutes.)

Sherwin excelled at running and participated in track and field events in high school. His father was very competitive and pressured him to race. His family often reminded him that Donavon Bailey, a retired sprinter who at one time held the world record for the 100-metre dash, was originally from their same area of Jamaica. Sherwin didn't mind the pressure because the only time he felt free and accepted was when he was running.

As Sherwin's body matured, he remained very lithe and lean, and found he was best suited to the middle-distance runs, the 800- and 1500-metre. As well, he competed in the 400-metre and the 400-metre relay.

There were only three high schools in Mandeville, so Sherwin frequently travelled to Kingston to race. He also competed at the Inter-Secondary Schools Sports Association Boys and Girls Athletics Championships, unofficially known as Champs. This is a yearly competition, and it is quite a big deal. Sherwin is very proud of the fact that Jamaica has produced some of the fastest men and women in the world.

Training, studying, and frequently functioning as the man of his household while his father was away occupied Sherwin throughout high school. The other boys his age simply assumed he was too busy for girls, or possibly too religious, and Sherwin didn't give anyone any reason to think otherwise. Besides, a gay athlete, especially a fast and powerful runner, would have been impossible for his friends to comprehend. Quite obviously, chi chi bwoys could never make good athletes in any sport.

Sherwin was sixteen when his world changed. He happened to be attending a track and field meet in Kingston. The beginning of the day was uneventful. He was casually stretching his legs on the sidelines of the track close to a well-known female athlete his age. This girl happened to have unusually large breasts, and most of the boys on his track team made lewd and inappropriate comments about her chest when watching her train and race; that day was no exception.

Another boy he did not know was standing very near to him on the sidelines, looking his way. Feeling obligated to comment about the female athlete close by, but not wanting to say anything vulgar or disrespectful, Sherwin made a benign comment to the other boy about the girl's enviable talent as a hurdler.

"I was looking at you," came the matter-of-fact response.

A jolt of electricity surged through Sherwin's body and his knees almost buckled. He had no idea what to say or even if he should say anything. He was not convinced that any words would emanate from his mouth should he try to speak. Flustered, Sherwin grinned sheepishly at the other boy, waved goodbye, and jogged off.

Much to his amazement, the boy jogged after him, caught up to Sherwin, and introduced himself. His name was Rajae, and he attended an all-boys' high school in Kingston. He was already in Sixth Form, the final two years of high school, which meant he was older than Sherwin.

Rajae stood a good eight inches taller than Sherwin, with a much broader frame. He had strong muscular legs and a very chiseled abdomen, which was noticeable even under his tee shirt. Sherwin said he was becoming aroused just looking at him. He was careful to maintain eye contact.

Like many of the taller boys, Rajae was a sprinter, competing in the 100-metre and 200-metre distances. He told Sherwin that he seldom placed in the top five, but he was a solid competitor. He remembers that Rajae sounded somewhat dejected when he told Sherwin that he had not been selected by the coach this year to run the 100-metre relay. Sherwin was not accustomed to boys being vulnerable and sharing their feelings, and he was really touched by Rajae's honesty.

They talked for what felt like an eternity. Conversation with Rajae was not like with any of Sherwin's other friends. Sherwin was riveted. It was easy and free, and felt authentic. Sherwin's heart raced the entire time. He didn't dare hope that Rajae was like him.

Far too soon, Sherwin had to go prepare for his 400-metre relay. Rajae gave him a quick good-luck hug, which was innocent enough. However, he let his hand gently brush against Sherwin's as they pulled apart. The intense look he gave Sherwin as they made physical contact told him that the hand stroke was not an accident. For Sherwin, it was the most sensual interaction he had ever experienced.

This simple caress of the hand marked the beginning of a beautiful, lifelong friendship.

Rajae eventually gave Sherwin his first real kiss and became his first lover. He introduced Sherwin to gay teenage meetups and the surreptitious world of queer life in Jamaica. Sherwin was surprised to learn just how many homosexual men lived in his country. He hadn't realized it because it was, and still is, so deeply hidden. Messages of homophobia were predominately what he was exposed to as a child, and much of the mainstream music in Jamaica, at least when he was living there, encouraged violence against gay people, especially feminine-looking men, regardless of their actual sexual orientation.

Rajae also educated Sherwin on the lives of marginalized gay and transgender people who had been stabbed, beaten, burned, raped, shot, and forced to leave home. Many lived in abandoned buildings or on the street. Sherwin was petrified of being outed and trying to survive on the streets. From Rajae, he learned discretion and self-preservation. He also discovered what it felt like to be truly loved. Rajae never apologized for being gay or for being attracted to other males. He was an intelligent, handsome, and physically powerful young man, and he was Sherwin's first gay role model.

Sherwin and Rajae never became boyfriends, but they hooked up whenever they could, at track and field meets, or whenever Sherwin could find an excuse to visit Kingston, or Rajae to Mandeville.

Rajae was a very masculine-looking boy from a wealthy family. He worked tirelessly on his schoolwork. For Rajae, going to university abroad was his ticket out of Jamaica and away from all the homophobia and the secret life he hated. He was quite a brilliant scholar, and helped Sherwin prepare for his A-level exams well in advance. Sherwin's family welcomed him into their home with open arms. His father thought that Rajae was a good influence on his son, focusing on school and track and field instead of partying and engaging in the reckless, ungodly, and foolish behaviour of many of the male teenagers. Rajae fit none of the stereotypes about how a homosexual man looked, walked, or talked. It would never even have entered Sherwin's father's mind that his son was engaging in sexual activities with this boy.

The very first time Sherwin visited Rajae in Kingston, he was stunned to learn that Rajae's family was aware of his sexuality, although it was never overtly discussed. Unlike any of the other families Sherwin knew, Rajae's family was quietly supportive of gay rights. Sherwin knew that his father would never be accepting let alone tolerant. Sherwin also believed that his entire family was oblivious to his sexual orientation, and he needed it to remain that way.

When Sherwin finished high school, he entered his first year at Northern Caribbean University (NCU) in Mandeville, a school affiliated with the Seventh-day Adventist Church. Students as well as faculty are expected to comply with the rules of the religion and conduct themselves in what would be considered a Christian manner.

Sherwin was extremely guarded and closeted at school because of its religious foundation, and he didn't want to draw any attention to himself. By now, Rajae was in his second year at the University of California, Los Angeles (UCLA). Sherwin was very lonely and isolated during his first few months of post-secondary education, and he desperately missed Rajae.

In early December of his Sherwin's freshman year, Rajae gifted his friend a plane ticket to LA so that they could be together over the holiday. They had been planning for Sherwin to visit LA since Rajae first left Jamaica. Sherwin had never travelled out of his country, and he was looking forward to it. However, he had one final assignment to complete before the December break, and he knew he had to focus.

Sherwin was absolutely delighted when at the end of class one day, two young women asked if he would like to collaborate with them. Sherwin immediately agreed. He was quite taken aback when another male student literally yanked him aside and told him that he should not work with those girls because they were *batty gyals* (derogatory term in Jamaican Patois for lesbians), which were nasty and unnatural.

Sherwin had no idea whether the girls were lesbians. And he really didn't care. He was on an emotional high thinking about going to LA. He just wanted to finish his work, and besides, it was encouraging to know that there might be other homosexual students at such a religious institution.

Sherwin thanked the student for his concern but reiterated to him the Seventh-day Adventist position that even if the girls were lesbian, God has compassion for homosexuals. The young man became enraged and accused Sherwin of being a batty bwoy himself, as well as a lover of dykes. Sherwin simply turned and walked away, which seemed to infuriate the young man even more.

As it turned out, the girls were not only lesbian, but they were in a romantic relationship. They kept a low profile at the university for obvious reasons. They also had two other roommates, which they believed helped them create a heterosexual façade. Sherwin ended up visiting their place numerous times to complete assignments.

The girls were bright and friendly, and Sherwin began to let his guard down. When they asked whether he had a girlfriend, he said he had no time to date. When they asked him whether he had a boyfriend, he avoided the question with a smile. But he didn't deny he was attracted to other males either. It never occurred to him that the roommates might talk, or that other students in his program were speculating about his sexuality, so he was completely unprepared for what was about to happen.

Late one night as he was leaving their place, several young men sprang out of nowhere carrying bats and sticks. Sherwin recognized the boy from his class who had accused him of being a lover of gay women. The men were ranting and screaming homophobic slurs. Their eyes were glazed and they looked like wild animals hunting for prey. There were at least four of them, but it happened so fast, Sherwin did not have time to count. He did notice that they were all larger than him.

The first hit came full force with a bat, which slammed against the right side of Sherwin's body. It almost knocked him to the ground. Pain seared through his shoulder and his ribs. The second blow was almost instantaneous, but with a much lighter stick. It struck Sherwin on the side of his head, and blood poured from his ear. He still remembers the taste of his blood and the feeling of his cheek swelling.

One of the men rushed up to the girls' door and started kicking it with his boot. Two of the others followed and began smashing the door with their bats. The girls inside of the house had already heard the commotion and had telephoned the police.

Another perpetrator swung at Sherwin with a metal rod. This time, Sherwin saw it coming. As the man pulled his arms back to swing, Sherwin responded like he would to the starting pistol at the beginning of a race. He took off so fast that the thugs were taken completely by surprise. Two or three of them chased after him, but even injured, Sherwin was too fast. He pulled away from the pack and ran to safety.

Sherwin hid behind some bushes trying to catch his breath, and then staggered home. He is not sure whether he lost consciousness. By the time he reached home, the police were already there. Sherwin's head pounded and his ear was ringing. He could not move his right shoulder.

The police asked Sherwin why he was visiting a "dyke house" (their words) and whether he observed anyone trying to bash their door down. Then they asked him whether he was a homosexual. Sherwin cannot remember whether he answered them, but he thinks he didn't say anything at all. They turned to his mother and told her that no good ever came of batty bwoys and that she would be wise to get her son into line. They also gave her the name of a place that could "convert" Sherwin and make him normal if necessary.

Sherwin's mother asked the police if they were going to press assault charges against Sherwin's attackers. They shook their heads no and suggested she pray for her son. They explained that one of the boys could be charged with vandalism for damaging the front door of the dyke house, but that homosexuals deserved whatever treatment they got. There was almost glee in their voices when they declared that the girls could not actually prove who had done the damage, so it was highly unlikely that any arrests would be made.

Sherwin was surprised to see that his mother held her tongue. She answered only the necessary questions as simply as she could and did not offer any additional information. When the police were done, one of his sisters politely escorted the officers out of the house. By now, everyone was crying. Sherwin was just grateful that his father was on the road. He learned much later that his mother had observed first-hand at the hospital the abuse of power as well as the treatment of homosexual men by some police officers. She had provided medical treatment to multiple men on numerous occasions who had experienced this abuse as well as other hate crimes. Sherwin learned that that is why his mother was so uncharacteristically quiet and careful with her answers. She did not want to antagonize the officers.

Sherwin's mother took pictures of his injuries before she cleaned them up and dressed them. She thought Sherwin should go to the hospital and see a doctor, but he refused. With tears in her eyes, she begged him not to return to Jamaica once he was in LA. She said that Jamaica was no place for a young, homosexual man. She told him that she knew Rajae loved him and would make sure he was safe. She also explained that she had been in touch with J-FLAG (Jamaica Forum for Lesbians, All-Sexuals and Gays) who had provided her with some information on receiving political asylum in the United States. Sherwin was too shocked and too weak to comment. He wondered how long his mother had known. Clearly it had been a while.

He and his mother held each other in a long embrace. His mother wept.

The very next day, Sherwin's mother carefully wrote and signed an account of his attack, the lack of police support, and the brutalization of other young men in Jamaica perceived to be gay. She wrote that as a nurse, she witnessed the sometimes-fatal results of this brutality. Other nurses who were colleagues anonymously corroborated these occurrences.

The students from the house where Sherwin had been doing schoolwork when the attack happened did the same. Sherwin explained to them that their testimonies might help him find safety. They were smart enough to know that Sherwin would need proof that his life was in danger if he remained in Jamaica. It didn't hurt that Brian Williamson's death that same year had been widely publicized and was on the radar of human rights activists in the country.

When Sherwin's father heard about the attack, he agreed with the police that his son should have known better than to hang out with a bunch of dykes. He also said that no son of his would be a batty man. He told Sherwin that if he was gay, or even if he supported people who were homosexual, he was no longer his son and he never wanted to see him again.

At the time of these interviews, Sherwin had not spoken to his father in thirteen years. He maintains contact with his mother and his sisters who love him and quietly tolerate his homosexuality. But they tell people Sherwin lives in Toronto because of career opportunities. They do not ever say that he is gay.

Shortly before his twentieth birthday, Sherwin entered Canada as a refugee. Rajae was convinced that Sherwin would have a greater chance of having his claim accepted in Canada rather than the United States, and he helped Rajae to research the process. He also signed an affidavit that he had been engaged in homosexual relations with Rajae for several years. As it isn't always easy to prove one's sexuality to the refugee board, Rajae was hell-bent on ensuring that Sherwin had all the proof that he needed.

Against protests, Rajae and his family gifted Sherwin a significant amount of money. Sherwin didn't know whether he would ever have the means to repay them. But Sherwin's mother was correct. Rajae told Sherwin he would love him forever, and the feeling was mutual.

Sherwin has been living in Toronto since first arriving in Canada as a refugee all those years ago. He does not volunteer much information about the early years of living here. He only mentions that the move, though welcome, was difficult. He does let me know that the very first June after he arrived, he proudly marched in Toronto's Pride Parade.

Sherwin's dream was to become a nurse, like his mother, and he beamed with pride when he told me at the time of his first interview that he had just recently been accepted into a degree nursing program at a local university. He had been working full-time as a Personal Support Worker, and part-time waiting tables in a restaurant for many years to save enough money for tuition.

Sherwin and Rajae have remained close friends over the years. Rajae lives in California (he is now a permanent resident) where he works in the movie industry. He travels quite frequently to Toronto for business and either stays with Sherwin, or they stay together in Rajae's usually lavish hotel room. Both men continue to run long distances daily. Sherwin feels he is the freest when he is running.

Sherwin believes that Rajae not only changed his life, but also saved it.

Once Sherwin stops speaking, I tell him that it sounds like he and Rajae are in a long-term relationship. Sherwin's dazzling smile lights up his entire face. "Perhaps," he says.

Sherwin will be forever grateful to Canada for welcoming him. He also expressed his thanks to the 519 Community Centre in Toronto for their support and guidance. He has made many friends in Toronto, especially a group of people from the Caribbean who are also gay. However, he misses the physical beauty of his country, the smell of the air, and the taste of the food. He knows that 2SLGBTQ+ people are by and large still not accepted, or even tolerated in his home country. This devastates him.

"I am Canadian, but I'm Jamaican too," he said.

When my dream of publishing this book finally became a reality, I contacted Sherwin to alert him to the fact that his story was finally going to be told. He was thrilled, and he updated me on his life. He is now a registered nurse working in a large hospital in Toronto, and he is studying part-time for his master's degree in nursing. He is interested in becoming a nurse practitioner, and he would like to specialize in working with people living with HIV/AIDS.

Sherwin, like almost everyone I interviewed, did not want his real name used in his story. He asked me to assign him a Jamaican-sounding pseudonym. I selected the name Sherwin, which means "swift" or "quick as the wind."

#

One year after Sherwin came to Canada, Jamaica was described in *Time* magazine as "the most homophobic place on earth.[13]" Certainly, the high rate of violence, including murder, targeting people with non-conventional sexual orientations or gender identities in Jamaica has been the focus of much attention from human rights activists and media over the years. Culturally, homosexuality is considered immoral and abhorrent in this country. It is not uncommon for young 2SLGBTQ+ people to be forced onto the streets when their families learn of their sexual orientation or gender identity. Gay bashing continues to occur, especially against males that are coded as feminine. Lesbians, on the other hand, are at risk of correctional rape, in the belief that sex with a man will cure them of what is believed to be perverse sexual desires, and make them whole again.

It is important to note that not everyone in the country thinks the same way, and Jamaica is certainly not alone in the Caribbean in its persecution of people who identify as 2SLGBTQ+. The cultural expectation in this area of the world that men should be hyper-masculine coupled with the view that heteronormativity is the only correct way for humans to exist are pervasive throughout most countries in the Caribbean. As a result, men who engage in sex with other men frequently keep it to themselves. They do not have anywhere to go for information and support, and consequently have a higher incidence and prevalence of HIV/AIDS than in many other areas of the world.

The oppression and violence in Jamaica must be considered within the context of the high levels of unemployment, poverty, and violence in the country. Sherwin referenced the intersection of poverty and being gay several times during his interview. For example, he told me that Brian Williamson's death was shocking because he could afford to live in a more exclusive area of the country. A gay person who is wealthy has a much greater chance of being tolerated, and a much lesser chance of experiencing violence than one who is barely surviving on the streets. This is the case in many countries around the world.

The situation in Jamaica has been slow to change, but there has been some movement forward. Health advocates have begun to challenge societal attitudes in the hope that this will help with the fight against HIV/AIDS and improve the availability and quality of services and care to the 2SLGBTQ+ communities. The harsh anti-sodomy laws in the country, which can put a man in jail for up to ten years, are believed to be one of the reasons why some men engaging in sexual activity with other men do not seek information and health care. 2SLGBTQ+ rights are very slowly emerging into political conversations.

In February of 2021, the Inter-American Commission on Human Rights demanded that Jamaica gather and report statistics on discriminatory and violent acts against people because of sexual orientation or gender identity, including aggression towards people who are intersex.[14]

Unfortunately, according to the organization J-FLAG, 2SLGBTQ+ people are still not very likely to report hate crimes directed at them because of low persecution rates and general mistrust of the police. J-FLAG has been calling on the censorship of music in Jamaica that is homophobic and promotes violence against people who are 2SLGBTQ+.

There is apparently some optimism among human rights activists that Jamaica wants to provide protection to all its citizens. Currently, same-sex marriage is not legal in Jamaica, but there are no censorship laws against discussing or even promoting 2SLGBTQ+ topics and serving openly in the military is permitted for people who have identified themselves as gay. Changing gender on documentation is also legal in the country, and surgery confirming their identified gender is not required to do so.

Moving forward, conversations around the construction of gender and gender roles in Jamaica would be helpful to the 2SLGBTQ+ communities (and anyone in the country). The apparent hate of "feminine" traits in men proves to be extremely detrimental to both men and women, as well as to people who are 2SLGBTQ+. Basic human rights and safety for people of all sexual orientations and gender identities need to be seen within the cultural context of the country and the people that live there.

In the Land of Wood and Water.

Sungai:
Trying to Wash the Gay Away

I was raised in a Catholic home, although I haven't identified with that religion for many years. If I am being honest, up until meeting Sungai, I naïvely believed that exorcisms in the church were a thing of the past, now relegated to horror movies and novels. Further, I thought that exorcisms were likely the only way that people hundreds of years ago had to treat complex mental health conditions they didn't understand, such as dissociative identity disorder, schizophrenia, or even physical disorders, such as epilepsy. In the absence of any real facts, the sufferers, who may well have displayed unexplained, uncontrollable behaviours, were believed to be possessed by the devil, and someone acting with the authority of a higher power was required to expel the evil spirits from within them. From my perspective, this was an archaic and barbaric ritual, and I was confident there wouldn't be a need for any exorcisms today.

Clearly, I was wrong. Sungai barely survived his exorcism. But now I am ahead of the story.

Unlike Sherwin, who had been in Canada many years at the time of his interview, when I met Sungai in 2023, he had only recently arrived in Toronto from Indonesia. He was early in the process and was waiting on a work permit as well as a date for his Refugee Claim Hearing. He was told to expect the work permit soon, but that his scheduled hearing would be around twenty months away.

Sungai is completely fluent in English, Indonesian, and Kupang Malay. For his interview, we met in a restaurant in Toronto's Greektown. Sungai was soft-spoken, but he was not shy. A petite young man, he is barely 5'5" tall with a very slight frame. He has straight black hair, and brown eyes, with clear, very light brown skin. Although he was twenty years old when we met, he appeared much younger, and could have easily passed as a boy of fourteen or fifteen, with no evidence of any facial hair.

Sungai was keen to share his story. He explained that he wanted other gay men, especially from his part of the world, to know that they were not alone and there was hope for a future as an openly homosexual man.

Sungai grew up in East Nusa Tenggara, the most southern province of Indonesia comprised of 500 or so islands. It's the only province in Indonesia where Catholicism is the majority religion, and his family are practicing Catholics. Sungai told me that although he lived there most of his life, he wasn't born there, and preferred not to share the location of his birth. For confidentiality and safety reasons, he provided very little information about his family. He mentioned only that they worked in the tourist industry and that they were very successful.

As a little boy, Sungai always assumed he would get married to a woman and have a family, although he didn't really spend much time thinking about it. He felt he was a regular kid, who hated doing his homework and preferred to play video games. His parents were very strict about homework, as was the school he attended. He practiced martial arts, and his favourite sports were badminton and volleyball. Nothing out of the ordinary. Sungai pointed out that he didn't fit the stereotype of gay men who enjoyed "girl" things as children. However, when he was eleven, he developed a crush on his best friend, which resulted in immense confusion and emotional turmoil for him.

I wanted to hug him when we met so we could be physically close, but Indonesians don't greet each other that way. When I was near him, my heart pounded a little faster. I wanted to reach out and touch his face. These feelings were strong, but I knew I couldn't do anything about it. One afternoon when we were playing badminton, I reached too far for the birdie and fell backwards to the ground. I fell hard. He ran over to check I was okay. When he pulled me up on my feet with my arms, I landed very close—face to face. He kissed me, or maybe I kissed him. I can't be sure, but it was my first kiss, and it felt like everything stopped moving.

Sungai said that after the kiss, neither of them said a word. His friend ran back to the other side of the net, and they finished their game. Sungai doesn't remember who won. He only remembered feeling very uncomfortable with what happened, but at the time, he didn't understand why. Maybe it was because he really liked the kiss, and he wished it would happen again. He had no idea what his friend thought because they never talked about feelings and neither of them ever mentioned the incident. It didn't seem to ruin their friendship, and they continued to be close. Outwardly, everything was just the same. But inside, Sungai began to have increasing thoughts about kissing other boys.

> I was really confused. I didn't understand my feelings or my
> reaction. I knew some people are gay. I just didn't want it to
> be me.

Sungai explained that where he grew up, there was a quiet, discrete gay presence, but it was largely hidden. It seemed to be tolerated by the broader community if it wasn't obvious. From Sungai's lived experience, he recognized that most gay people don't ever come out to their families. They quietly exist but continue to participate in family events under the guise that they are heterosexual. Families seem to assume that all their relatives and close friends are straight. I learned that the estimated population of Indonesia in 2023 was 277,534,122. For the sake of argument, if we assume that four percent of the population is gay (and that number is likely higher) and maybe another one percent is transgender, there are conservatively over thirteen million people who are not "out" in Indonesia. That is one *massive* closet!

Since his country is religious, Sungai believes that, if asked, most people would say that anyone who identifies as 2SLGBTQ+ is a deviant and goes against the word of God. Further, many of them still believe that 2SLGBTQ+ people are mentally ill and need intervention to be cured.

As Sungai went through puberty, he recognized that he was probably gay, but he had no one to talk to about it. His badminton friend seemed to be content to ignore what had happened when they were younger. At church, Sungai prayed hard to be made straight, but despite his efforts, nothing seemed to change. He told me he was full of self-loathing during this time.

> Praying wasn't helping so I went to confession. I told the
> priest I was having sex thoughts about other boys and begged
> for forgiveness. The priest said I didn't need to be forgiven

as much as I needed to be saved. He told me I needed thirty days of serious prayer to be released from my unclean and sinful desires. He said there was a facility that could help me and encouraged me to tell my family. Several months later, after weeks of agonizing and not sleeping very well, I did.

Sungai's parents were devastated when he told them he was attracted to other boys. They interrogated him about whether he had ever acted on these impulses. He told them he had not. He convinced himself it wasn't a lie to avoid mentioning the kiss on the badminton court. Afterall, he was only a child at the time, and it was just a simple kiss. His parents were relieved. They forbade him from discussing the situation with his friends or siblings. Sungai got the impression that his parents were more concerned about embarrassing the family than his well-being. He told them what the priest had said about the intensive prayer. They arranged a meeting with one priest from their church where Sungai agreed to spend thirty days at a special prayer facility that could cure him. He was just shy of his seventeenth birthday at the time. Sungai was not afraid to go. He really did not want to be gay. And thirty days of praying did not seem so terrible or difficult.

At the facility, Sungai was expected to pray on his knees on a hard floor for many hours each day. It was mainly teenage boys and young men in attendance, but there were a few girls. The dorms where they stayed at the facility were segregated by gender. Sungai was placed in a room with another boy about his age, who had already been there for two weeks. They were given restricted amounts of food to eat and were not permitted any access to technology or the internet. There were no visitors allowed, not even parents. They were constantly monitored. Showers were timed and supervised. They were warned about the sin of masturbation. Not exactly a five-star accommodation, but not completely awful either.

According to Sungai, the isolation, and the complete lack of privacy were the most challenging aspects for him.

Between the long prayer sessions, there was mandatory group therapy as well as individual counselling. During group, they were repeatedly told that they could become heterosexual if they wanted, if their prayers were sincere. Several times the group was visited by people who alleged that they used to be homosexual, but were now happily "normal," because God had cured them. Most of these visitors stressed that they were in conventional heterosexual marriages, as if being married to someone of the opposite sex proved that they weren't gay.

Sungai's descriptions of group sessions baffled me and much of what he said that occurred defies any logic. He explained that during these sessions, they were first taught then practiced very stereotypical ways that men and women should walk, talk, and behave, and he thought this was both ignorant and stupid. He didn't understand what walking had to do with sexuality and I agreed with him without reservation. He also said that boys who were feminine in any way were repeatedly bullied and humiliated in front of everyone.

Sungai did not speak during group unless he was specifically addressed. He mostly listened and complied with what was requested. He questioned to himself the purpose of the group and the group activities, but he kept his opinions to himself. Sungai has a very scientific and logical mind, and he felt that the information being disseminated about gender and sexuality seemed to be completely devoid of fact.

However, during his individual counselling sessions, the "therapist" (Sungai doesn't know if the person had any qualifications) told him to be honest and that he would have a better chance of being cured if he actively participated in the sessions. Sungai really wanted to become heterosexual, so he approached the first few meetings with sincerity. The counsellor showed him nude pictures of men and women and asked him which pictures he preferred. Sungai made the mistake of telling the truth. The counsellor told Sungai that he must pray harder, and that he might need medication to help curb his same-sex feelings if they did not start to dissipate. Sungai began to wonder if this was true and whether drug therapy was a viable option for him.

Sungai learned from his roommate that several of the boys in attendance had been there before. He warned Sungai to do everything that those in charge asked. He also told Sungai he should lie if they questioned him about whether his sexual attraction to men was waning. The roommate explained that if anyone displayed either "defiant" behaviour (meaning gender non-conforming) or persistent homosexual desires, they could be physically beaten, and in more extreme cases, might be administered electroconvulsive or shock therapy. Sungai didn't initially believe that a place recommended by his community priest would ever do those things and he thought maybe his roommate was exaggerating. He did appear to be overly dramatic.

Shortly after Sungai's roommate had warned him about what could happen to people who did not comply, a new boy entered the facility who was younger than Sungai. He was rude and outspoken during his first group session, swearing, and telling the group facilitators that the entire thing was a waste of time. The boy was repeatedly and sternly warned to stop using offensive and unholy language and to keep quiet, but his behaviour continued to escalate. Right in the middle of the group session, the facilitators physically restrained the boy and cuffed him to his chair. Then, one of them took a wooden paddle and repeatedly struck him on his back, torso, legs, and arms, until he was bleeding through his clothing. His screams were terrifying, and he begged the counsellor over and over to stop. He shouted "please" in between shrieks of pain. His shouts grew weaker and less, and then they eventually stopped. Sungai doesn't know if the boy was exhausted, unconscious, or dead. Then they uncuffed the boy from his chair and literally dragged him out of the room. Sungai never saw that boy again, nor was the incident ever mentioned. However, the message to all the participants about compliance, or perhaps submission, was received. Clearly, this wasn't just a place of prayer and Sungai was jolted into considering the very real possibility that what his roommate had said about other treatments or punishments that were administered could be true.

That night, when they thought everyone was asleep, Sungai and his roommate whispered about what they had witnessed in group. They didn't even know if the boy had lived. Sungai was physically shaking with fear. His roommate shared that he was almost eighteen, and as soon as he was legally an adult, he was going to flee from his family. He knew he was gay, he didn't want to change, and he wanted to live in a country where he could be free.

Sungai could not imagine life without his family, and since he only had to remain in the institution for twenty more days, he decided to go along with everything he was asked. By the end, he was telling his therapist that all his sinful feelings had left him, and he was happy to be made into a healthy and godly person. He hated lying but didn't want to risk confrontation or worse. He especially did not want to be returned to the prayer facility.

According to Sungai, the only thing that the experience in the prayer facility succeeded in doing was confirming for him that he was indeed a homosexual, and this was never going to change. It also hammered into him the belief that coming out of the closet was not an option. After he completed the thirty days, Sungai returned to his family.

Once Sungai returned home from his thirty days of prayer, he pretended he was now cured of any homosexual tendencies, and everything was fine. He was extremely stressed trying to catch-up with the schoolwork he had missed before writing his final exams and he tried to block the experience from his mind. Unfortunately, he had difficulty sleeping and kept waking up in the night sweating and shouting as he remembered watching the severe beating of the unnamed boy. He also blamed himself for being a coward and not intervening to stop the attack. He wondered if the boy had died meant that made him a witness to a murder. He became overwhelmed with these feelings and felt he couldn't continue to live with the lie that he was straight. He was so overcome with guilt and shame that he felt like he might explode. When his parents questioned him about what was wrong, and why he was crying out in terror in his sleep, Sungai poured out the entire truth to them. Devastated, Sungai's parents turned to the church once again for advice.

The priest vehemently denied that anything violent would ever have happened at the prayer facility and told Sungai's parents that he was lying, just like he had lied when he claimed he was cured. Returning to the facility for more intensive prayer was no longer an option because the COVID pandemic had hit and, like most other places, the facility was closed. The priest advised that he feared Sungai had evil spirits inside of him that were screaming through him at night, and that it was the work of the devil that the thirty days of prayer had no impact on his deviant sexual urges. He concluded that Sungai would benefit from an exorcism. Sungai's parents were desperate to fix their son, so they agreed to the ritual, but they never communicated their plan to Sungai.

Without any explanation and seemingly out of the blue, Sungai's father drove him to the church. While he was confused, he had been taught not to question his father. There were no in-person services or meetings being held because of COVID protocols in the country. Sungai didn't recognize or understand that he was going to be exorcised until it was too late, and he never consented to the ritual. His father was not allowed to watch, and Sungai believes, even if he was present, he wouldn't have intervened.

Sungai doubts that what he experienced was a legitimate church-sanctioned exorcism because there is a strict protocol that must be followed for this to occur. Catholic Canon law mandates that an exorcism cannot be performed until the person believed to be possessed by the devil receives a thorough medical exam, and mental illness as a cause of the behaviours must be ruled out. Sungai never received any type of medical examination before the ritual took place, not even an interview. Permission from a bishop for the exorcism must be obtained beforehand. To Sungai's knowledge, nobody communicated anything to a bishop or anyone higher in the church than his local priests. According to the Catholic Church itself, very few priests have the specialized training that is required to perform the ritual and it seems unlikely that two of his parish priests would have had this specialized instruction.

What I have learned from briefly researching this topic is that in a church-sanctioned exorcism, there is never supposed to be any violent contact.[15] The purpose of an exorcism is to expel the devil from the person, not to torture them, punish them, or cause them harm. That was not Sungai's experience.

During a church-sanctioned exorcism, holy water is sprinkled on the person almost like a Baptism renewal. But in Sungai's case, after a few prayers, he was tied down, a rag was shoved into his mouth and a cloth was placed over his face. Large amounts of water from a bucket were repeatedly poured over his face, including his nose. He struggled to breath, repeatedly choking and gagging, but was unable to gasp for air because his mouth was blocked. This continued for an undermined length of time, and Sungai genuinely believed he was going to drown. The water continued pouring over him until he lost consciousness. When he awoke, his face was uncovered, and the rag had been removed from his mouth. One of the priests was beating him with a stick, commanding that the evil spirits leave his body. The other priest prayed over him holding rosary beads. What he was saying appeared to be scripted, but he was not reading from a book or a bible. Sungai does not remember much of what was chanted. He was shivering from pain, fear, and cold.

> My body was broken and weak, but this cruelty only made my belief in myself stronger. Maybe it was adrenalin, maybe something else. I felt extreme pain, but my mind seemed clearer. I knew I wasn't possessed, and I knew I wasn't deviant. What these priests did to me was wrong. They should be in jail.

Sungai is correct in his assertion. The "exorcism" he received while technically still a child, under the guise of a religious ritual, was barbaric and inhumane, and under international law, illegal. One-hundred and sixty-five countries, including Indonesia, have signed the United Nations Convention against Torture (and other cruel, degrading, and inhumane treatment)[16] although many of these same countries continue these practices when it comes to people who are 2SLGBTQ+. There doesn't seem to be any public outcry or any repercussions.

When it was over, the priests cleaned and dressed his wounds, removed the now soaked robe he had been given to wear, and returned his clothes. Sungai thanked the priests for saving him, even though the words were bitter in his mouth. He could barely walk to meet his father and fell into his arms when he saw him. His father essentially carried him to the car.

When they returned home that same evening, his parents never asked him about the exorcism. It seems extremely bizarre to me that they wouldn't want to talk about it, but Sungai said he was not even remotely surprised. His parents never talked about feelings. Even though he was traumatized, he had to push the memory of the experience aside so he could function. He turned his focus on preparing for final exams. He needed to achieve excellent grades as this was leading into his last year of high school, preparing him for university.

Because of the pandemic, his completion of upper secondary school was going to be virtual from home. Sungai's great attention to schoolwork seemed to placate his parents. They were thrilled by his behaviour and believed that their son had been cured. After the exorcism had occurred, Sungai recognized deep down that he had to find a way to leave Indonesia and his family. But he was still just a kid and had no significant money of his own. He knew he needed to play the long game.

Sungai's classmates would not have suspected he was gay based on being sexually inactive even if his last year of high school had been in-person, because that was the norm. People apparently do not kiss in public in Indonesia and sexual activity among teenagers is extremely rare because it is essentially forbidden. Sex or sex acts of any kind are never mentioned or discussed within most families, and they are certainly not an open topic of conversation at school. Because of the pandemic, dating or even socializing with girls was not an option, so Sungai didn't even have to pretend that he liked them. He spent all his time at home in front of a computer studying. Finally, something positive from that horrible virus!

Sungai longed to meet other gay boys for friendship and support. He knew he would be unable to access any reading materials because the risk of being caught by his family was too high. However, he secretly joined an online gay support group, which he accessed using a VPN that encrypted the connection between the device being used and the remote server. As a result, data he sent and received remained private. His IP address was hidden, and he was assigned a different one so that his real location was not disclosed.

I was relieved to learn Sungai never got caught attending this online group. He said it was very easy for him to pull off since all his schoolwork, including group work was virtual. He also shared that the hook-up app for gay men called Grindr was blocked in Indonesia but could also be accessed using a VPN, which bypasses the block and protects the person from discloser at the same time.

When it was time for university selection, Sungai's parents insisted that he apply to the Christian University of Indonesia (UKI, or Universitas Kristen Indonesia) in Jakarta, where successful students can enter medicine directly from high school. But Sungai didn't want to become a doctor, he wanted to be an engineer. And he wanted to attend the University in Melbourne, Australia, which is near his country, but has more acceptance for people who are 2SLGBTQ+. Melbourne is a vibrant and multicultural city. In Sungai's view, intolerance and hatred of gay people was rapidly rising in Indonesia, and he didn't feel safe. Homosexuality was becoming more overtly criticized and he was viewing more hate crimes and violence directed against 2SLGBTQ+ people in the media.

I told my parents I would agree to study medicine and forego my dream to be an engineer if I could attend the University of Melbourne [in Australia]. They were reluctant but after some coaxing, [they] agreed. According to them, I was an ideal son and student during my last year of high school.

Sungai completed his first year in biomedical sciences from Melbourne University. Unfortunately, it was completely online because of the pandemic and Sungai was once again stuck at home. Australia had one of the strictest border restrictions in the world. It didn't open its borders until February 2022, when Sungai was about to begin his second year. Unlike North America where the school year begins at the end of August or the beginning of September, a university's first semester in Australia begins in February or March and ends in June.

When he finally arrived in Melbourne, Sungai quietly investigated the possibility of seeking asylum there. He was devastated to learn that Australia had a huge backlog of refugees and the wait times for processing could be years. Sungai couldn't wait that long, so this didn't seem like a viable option, and he did not pursue it.

Also, while at university, Sungai realized that the prayer facility he attended while in high school was a form of conversion therapy. But at the time, he didn't understand this, and he was unfamiliar with either the term or the concept. The use of conversion therapy is a human rights violation that is both harmful and humiliating. There's no scientific evidence that attempting to alter a person's sexual orientation, gender identity, or gender expression works, and in many cases, the techniques used are forms of torture, which place the lives of people who are 2SLGBTQ+ in danger.[17] In 2020, the United Nations called for an international end to this practice.[17] Most countries have not acted on this recommendation. Canada passed Bill C-4 in January 2022, which banned conversion therapy across the country.

After recognizing that remaining in Australia as a refugee was not a good option for him, Sungai carefully researched how to seek asylum elsewhere in the world. He desperately wanted to seek refuge from the oppressive and dangerous life he knew he would have been forced to live had he remained in his home country, but he didn't want to make any quick or ill-informed decisions. Sungai certainly did his homework. He learned that both Canada and the United States were viewed quite positively in terms of 2SLGBTQ+ rights and safety, and they were also countries where English was spoken. One thing he discovered was that Canada was much more likely than most countries, including the United States, to grant him reciprocity for university credits he had already earned, and he thought that might be an important consideration somewhere down the road. He knew it would probably be a very long time before he might have the opportunity to continue his education, but he noted that the University of Toronto website mentioned an Indonesian student association. This gave Sungai comfort knowing that there would be other people his age from his part of Asia living there.

After Sungai set his target on Canada, he sourced information online about becoming a refugee. He discovered that it was possible to make a port of entry claim as soon as he arrived in Canada and that he should prepare as much documentation as possible ahead of travel to support his story. He also downloaded the Basis of Claim (BOC) form so that he could begin completing this mandatory form before his arrival.

Sungai waited patiently for his opportunity, and it finally presented itself. During the few weeks off between his first and second semester of his second year of university, Sungai returned home for the break. He succeeded in convincing his parents that they should transfer him all the money for his tuition, food, lodging, etc. for the entire semester. He felt he was responsible enough to establish and follow a budget and he told them he was striving to obtain some independence. Sungai's parents thought this was a wonderful stepping-stone to him behaving as an adult and agreed. They told him they were proud of him.

Instead of using the money for school, Sungai purchased a one-way ticket to Toronto, which left him with a significant amount of available funds. As far as his family knew, he was returning to the University in Melbourne to continue his studies. By the time they realized he had not returned to Melbourne, Sungai was already a refugee in Canada.

When we met, Sungai was staying with a host family that welcomed new refugees for their first few months in the country.

Sungai has no idea why he was so lucky. He was fortunate enough to be referred to a program that facilitated hosts for refugees. He understood that most people are sent to stay at homeless shelters when they arrive, but he only spent two nights in an emergency shelter before he was placed with his host. People who host refugees are put through a rigorous assessment before being accepted, so even though he was nervous to be taken into the home of a stranger, Sungai was exhausted, and felt that he was probably safe. He said he feels both lucky and grateful to have this arrangement. His host family has been generous and emotionally supportive and seems to have no issue whatsoever having open conversations about people with non-conventional sexual orientations or gender identities.

Unlike some of the other people I have interviewed, Sungai did not encounter any struggles or glitches with the process of becoming a refugee. He is fluent in English, which certainly helped, and he was prepared for what to expect. When he landed at the airport, they confirmed his identity, took his picture, and fingerprinted him. Sungai expected to be provided with an interview date, but the immigration officer interviewed him on the same day as his arrival. It was decided at the Toronto airport by the Canadian Border Service Agency (CBSA) officer that he was eligible to submit a refugee claim. But as prepared as he believed he was, Sungai was overcome with emotion when he first met with the CBSA officer, and he broke down and cried. He had not anticipated the overwhelming depth of loss that engulfed him with the realization that he had left his family and his home, and he may not see them for a very long time. Maybe even forever. He found the CBSA person to be both gentle and kind.

A few weeks after arriving in Toronto, Sungai contacted his family in Indonesia to let them know he was safe. His father told him not to return home until he was ready and willing to renounce his homosexuality. He also made it clear that no further financial support would be provided to Sungai unless he became straight, and that he should feel fortunate that his parents were not charging him for stealing their money. His mother thinks maybe he should try another exorcism and that he could have a happy life if only he prayed harder to eradicate his deviant urges. His parents refused to let him speak to his siblings and he doesn't know if they have any idea what he has been through. Sungai hopes that one day he will see his parents and siblings again. But it won't be any time soon.

Sungai shared with me that he battles his own biases against some men who are homosexual. He continues to be somewhat uncomfortable around flamboyant gay men or men that are very feminine in presentation. He recognizes this probably stems from his upbringing, and he is working on acceptance. He doesn't want to react in this way.

I am completely in awe of the courage and fortitude Sungai must possess to have fled his country and his family so that he could be safe and live an authentic life. I cannot even begin to imagine what he has endured and how difficult this must have been for him. And his journey is just beginning.

I asked him what name he would like me to use when telling his story. He told me he had been thinking about it since we had first met, and he selected the name Sungai. He explained, "It means river or stream in Indonesian. They tried to wash away the gay, but they failed. I was born gay, and nothing will change it."

As of February 2024, Sungai was still awaiting his hearing with the Immigration and Refugee Board of Canada. They told him that it would likely occur within 20 months of his arrival, but he has learned from others that the wait can be longer. He received his work permit not long after his arrival and he is currently working in the restaurant industry.

#

From my perspective, the situation in Indonesia for people with non-conventional sexual orientations or gender identities is both complex and confusing. Homosexuality is not technically against the law there, apart from the province of Aceh, which has been legally permitted to practice Islamic Shariah law. There, being gay is punishable by flogging, often in public, or by imprisonment. Although "cross-dressing" is apparently not prohibited under Qanun law, transgender people, especially trans women in Aceh, are often targeted by police who have reportedly cut their hair, forced them into male clothing, and detained them for training on becoming a real man. This is not only cruel but is clearly a violation of their human rights.

Even though being gay is not against the law in Indonesia, there is no protection for couples who are gay. Gay marriage is not recognized, and same-sex partners do not have access to couple's benefits through work. They are prevented from adopting a child. However, in Indonesia, someone who is single is permitted to adopt, which does create somewhat of a loophole. Presumably a person who is gay would be permitted to adopt a child if they are perceived as being single, and not in a same-sex relationship. In terms of reproductive rights, women known to be lesbian are not permitted access to reproductive technology to get pregnant.

In the past, Indonesia permitted same-sex sexual activity between consenting adults over eighteen if it occurred in private. However, in 2022, the Indonesia parliament passed a new criminal code which stated that sex outside of marriage, even if it is consensual, is a criminal offense.[18] This essentially renders it illegal for gay people to engage in sex, because people who are gay are not permitted to marry under Indonesian law. It isn't clear how they intend to police this.

The Constitution in Indonesia does not specifically speak to sexual orientation or gender identity, although it is supposed to guarantee everyone equality before the law, humane treatment at their job, religious freedom, freedom of expression, and other various legal rights. But at the same time, the government has banned websites and censored films that have gay content, and some people who are gay have been fired from the military.

Indonesia has historically been more accepting of people who are transgender, than of people with different sexual orientations. Many people who are transgender have been successful at legally changing their name and gender marker on official documents. However, over the last few years, there has been an uprise in conservative views, which has resulted in an increase in persecution of people who are 2SLGBTQ+, an increase in abusive police action, and a much greater occurrence of vigilantism against people with non-conventional sexual orientations or gender identities. Generally, there has been a widespread increase in discrimination against any 2SLGBTQ+ people residing there.

At the end of the day, if one assumes Sungai's viewpoint, it doesn't really matter what the government in Indonesia says or does. The pull of social, religious, and cultural beliefs is strong in this country. Some politicians have endorsed the rising hatred against people who are 2SLGBTQ+ to gain popularity and increase their support, especially with their most religious constituents. The country is heavily populated by people who believe that homosexuals are deviants and will morally corrupt the country if allowed to live their unconventional and abhorrent existence. There has been a co-ordinated attempt by some people to pressure the government into making homosexual acts punishable by death, based on religious beliefs. Thankfully, this more radical movement has not succeeded in their efforts. At least not yet.

It is no wonder Sungai did not feel safe in his home country. He wasn't.

Ariella:
Nobody's Princess

Sherwin introduced me to Ariella, the only transgender person that I interviewed who permitted me to tell her story. One other transgender person I spoke with who came to Canada as a refugee and is a friend of Ariella's, declined to be interviewed. They (preferred pronoun) continue to fear for their safety and complete anonymity is critical for them. However, they did accompany Ariella to her first appointment with me. I met with Ariella on three occasions, and she did permit me to record sections of her interview.

Ariella was identified as male at birth. She was born in a very poor region of Nigeria to a family with eight children that existed on only one or two dollars a day. The official language in Nigeria is English, but Ariella's family spoke Hausa in their home. Unlike many families in the area where she lived, they usually had some food to eat, but they had no running water and no washroom facilities. Many of Ariella's friends dropped out of school to beg on the streets or to find other ways of making money for their family's survival. But this was not why Ariella ended up there.

As a young child, I imagine I am a princess. I dream to marry a handsome prince. I have four sisters. Whenever I borrow their clothes, and my mother finds out, she beats me with horsewhip. I ask her why. She tells me I have the parts of man, and men cannot be princesses. I feel confused. I am not a boy. I am a girl. I know I will be a real princess one day.

The other children, especially her three brothers, were ruthless. They teased her relentlessly because of the way she moved. They accused her of walking and talking like a girl. They imitated her walk, as did the other children that lived near her. Sometimes they called her a f*g.

One day, awful day, my mother asks if I like boys. I tell her yes. She whips me until I can barely stand and tells me to leave the house. Never come back again. I have no money and no food. Only clothes I am wearing.

Ariella was thirteen when she was first thrown out onto the streets. Her mother assumed she was a homosexual when she answered honestly that she liked boys. Although she was telling the truth, this did not mean she was gay. She was a girl trapped inside of a boy's body. Girls were supposed to like boys and that is exactly what she said. Ariella didn't believe she was breaking any of her family's rules. She was devastated.

When she was first banished from her home, some of her sisters would sneak what little food they could out of the house and bring it to her. But when her mother found out, those siblings were not given any food for two days. So, it didn't take long before they stopped looking for her.

There are many children on the street. Some like me live there. Some work but go home at dark. I first make money by packing garbage. Then, when I get enough money, I buy trinkets to sell on the streets or in the outdoor markets. Many children on the street steal cellphones. I don't want to steal. I am not a thief. Sometimes gangs of kids steal my wares and I have to start with garbage again.

Ariella occasionally worked as a drug runner. A guy everyone on the street called "The Man" would come to the bridge where she lived and give her bags of drugs, mostly cocaine and marijuana, which she would strap under her shirt and then run it somewhere. The location of the drop changed continuously.

Ariella never did drugs. She had seen too many deaths on the street and too many strung-out children. Many of the children who used drugs were sick and dying, and Ariella did not want to die. Besides, drugs cost money, which was very hard to come by.

Ariella figured out that if she skimmed just a tiny amount of the drug from each bag, not sufficient to change the weight noticeably, she would have enough for a small package after five or six runs. These packages were like gold. She kept one hundred percent of whatever she got when they were sold. This system worked well for Ariella for a very long time, until she got caught.

I must have sold one of my packages to a rat. Or maybe the packages are light. The Man comes to find me under the bridge. He is not alone. There is another very large man with him, like a bodyguard. He is holding a pop bottle. I see he has a pistol. The Man beats me and the other man watches. The beating is okay. Home with horsewhip is worse.

Bodyguard man grabs me and tugs off my pants. He holds me down. I try to fight but, no use. The Man, I am sorry to have to tell you this, shoves the bottle in and out of my ass.

> I scream in pain. They are laughing. The Man says if I steal
> his drugs or money again, I am dead.

Ariella told me it was several weeks before she started to feel better. She also said that she felt very lucky. Some of the other children sleeping under the bridge helped her with her wounds. Instead of pocketing her things, they brought her food and water. They helped her walk and tried to clean her from the bleeding.

When Ariella started to feel well enough to work, the street children were all abuzz with information. Aid workers were coming to take the street kids somewhere safe. It was a government social welfare program, or something. But apparently their priority was the younger ones; those under fourteen. The children wanting shelter were supposed to bring their belongings and meet at a designated time and place.

At sixteen, Ariella had already been on the street for three years. But she was small for her age, likely from malnourishment, and looked much younger. So, she decided she would tell them she was fourteen and see what happened. The truth was, she was completely exhausted. Her body was covered in bruises, and she had been repeatedly raped on the streets. Not all her cuts had healed, and it still hurt when she needed to have a bowel movement. Ariella longed for somewhere softer to sleep.

> The two men who meet us are not Nigerian. They are white
> and accents when they speak English. Most of the time, they
> speak a different language. I think French.

First, the children were given food while their names and birthdates were recorded on a clipboard. Ariella remembers how startled all of them were that the food was hot. Then they were asked to climb into the back of a very large van. It was not overly cramped, even though there were seven of them. Five girls, one boy, and Ariella.

The girls were young, probably not more than eleven or twelve. Ariella had sisters that age. None of them looked familiar, but there were literally dozens of children living and working on the streets. Ariella recognized the boy. She had seen him turning tricks in the alleyway near the market. Ariella was sceptical that this boy was only fourteen, but it was none of her business, and she was certainly not in any position to judge.

The van made one stop at a gas station, and the children were offered a washroom break and something cold to drink. From what Ariella could see, it all appeared legitimate. They drove for about two hours to a large city in one of the northern states. Once they were there, they were taken to a hotel.

There are other little girls here. The men say they will bring some girls to a foster home in Switzerland. I am sick in my stomach. Foreigners who foster street kids sell them for cheap workers or sex. The men line the girls up. They pick six or seven girls who look young and pretty. Now I know for sure. They will sell them for sex or maybe for sex movies.

The remaining children were told they would be placed in people's homes. They would be safe and off the street in exchange for helping around the house. By now the children were stealing glances with each other, communicating both fear and uncertainty with their eyes. But they were all silent.

Ariella broke that silence. She asked if they would be paid for their work. "You will be part of a family," came the curt reply.

I stand up and walk right over to the men. I ask what kind of work we must do. I ask if we can go to school. The men look at me like I am crazy. One of them shouts. He calls me stupid f*ggot. I tell him I am not a f*g. I call him mumu (Nigerian word for idiot). The other man slaps me across the face. I say I would rather die than be sold as a slave.

The man who had slapped Ariella responded by punching her in the stomach. When she collapsed to the floor, he kicked her over and over, with full force. Instinctively, Ariella curled up into a ball and put her arms over her head. The only boy in the room jumped onto the man's back and tried to pull him away. But the second man grabbed him and hurled him across the room. Ariella heard the sickening sound of the boy smashing against the wall and then crashing to the floor. Now both men were repeatedly kicking at Ariella's body. The blows hit her back, legs, arms, and head.

The last thing Ariella remembers is hearing the terrified screams of all those little girls: "I can still hear their cries now, at night, alone and it's quiet. I try to forget, but I cannot."

Ariella woke up in a laneway, tossed away like a bag of garbage and presumably left there to die. It hurt her to breathe. Her clothes were torn and bloody. Some of her more recent wounds had re-opened. She was in so much pain, she couldn't move, but at least she was in a large city. She remembers thinking that it would be easier to find street work here than in the smaller villages. She fell in and out of sleep. Or maybe it was in and out of consciousness.

An *ashewo* (a Nigerian word for prostitute) named Chisimdi discovered Ariella the next morning when she was taking out the trash. Chisimdi initially thought that Ariella was dead when she saw her lying there. She told Ariella that she had to put her hand on her chest to determine whether she was breathing. When she realized Ariella was still alive, she ran back into her house for help. Chisimdi and the other ashewo carried Ariella into their apartment. They cared for her themselves because they were afraid to seek medical attention. They didn't want to be exposed to the authorities and thrown into prison. This time, it was almost two months before Ariella was recovered enough from her injuries to move around.

Chisimdi and the others were sex-workers, but they were not on the streets. They did most of their work in the area's hotels. Their clients were often tourists or men in the city for business. These men were seldom violent. And they always paid their money upfront.

Chisimdi and the other girls fell in love with Ariella. They loved her shrieks of delight when she was trying on their prostitute outfits. She paraded around the house in makeup and heels, and offered them unsolicited advice on what to wear. Chisimdi and the girls assumed that Ariella was a young, gay boy.

In the beginning, Ariella slept in Chisimdi's room. After a time, one of the roommates moved out, so Ariella acquired that room. She began to pay for her share of the food, and occasionally pitched in with rent money when she could afford it. She also assumed responsibility in the house for grocery shopping, and food preparation. The other girls would give her money, and she would take it to the market and shop. Ariella enjoyed being in the kitchen and loved to cook: "I never cooked that way before. My family has no stove. It is very exciting."

For money, Ariella gave blowjobs near the hotel where Chisimdi entertained her Johns. Ariella also found that if she hung around near the film house later in the evening, she would find business. Ariella dressed as a boy for work. The younger the men thought she was, the higher she was paid. Chisimdi showed her how to trim her underarm and pubic hair really short, so she looked like a younger boy.

Ariella didn't mind the work. It was easier and less painful than the work she did when she was on the street near her family. At least here she was never raped or beaten.

Ariella remained with Chisimdi for over two years. The faces of some of the roommates changed. But Chisimdi was a constant. She became the only stable and loving adult Ariella had ever had in her life. It had taken a year before Ariella was able to sleep through the night. Chisimdi would come into Ariella's bed and comfort her when she screamed in her sleep, which was very often.

Chisimdi was the first one Ariella ever told that although she was attracted to boys, she was not gay. She felt she was not a boy, but a girl, who was somehow living in a boy's body.

"I don't dress-up in girl's clothes. I am a girl."

Chisimdi knew two other transgender women and she introduced them to Ariella. They were both sex workers, but unlike Chisimdi, they were on the street. It gave Ariella great comfort to know that she was not the only person in the world who felt the same way. But she wondered if it was possible for a transgender woman to exist off the streets. To have a real life. To maybe live with a man and somehow have a family.

> The trans women here are nice. They explain about hormone drugs and surgery for my bottom. I am so surprised. It sounds unreal, like films people talk about. I don't have much money and the drugs to fix my body are expensive. They tell me about a place to go with no doctors where drugs are cheap. I really want breasts. Chisimdi tells me the place is dangerous. She does not want me to go there.

Ariella and Chisimdi developed a very close and loving relationship. Ariella was completely comfortable with her. Up until now, nobody had ever bothered to ask Ariella how she felt, and even if she would have volunteered the information, no one would have listened. But Chisimdi always listened. Ariella was lulled into a false sense of security living with her. She thought that the difficult part of her

life was over. After a time, Ariella began to dress as a woman outside
of the house, unless she was working.

The first time Ariella was caught by the police dressed as a
woman, they beat her with clubs and told her to disappear. One
suggested she kill herself. The second time she was arrested, she
would have been jailed for committing the indecent act of wearing
women's clothing, but Chisimdi bribed the police officers with
money. Ariella was able to come home.

But now, Chisimdi and her roommates were at risk of being
targeted for providing lodging and protection for a supposed
homosexual. Chisimdi was afraid for her safety, and for the safety
of her roommates. They could not afford to be harassed by police,
and they feared going to jail. Ariella offered to move out.

Chisimdi did not want Ariella to leave. She confessed to Ariella
that when she found her in the alleyway, it wasn't just her injuries
that were horrendous. Chisimdi had been completely shocked by
how skeletally thin and frail that Ariella looked. Now, she loved
Ariella like a younger sister and Ariella loved her back. Chisimdi
never had much of a family life or childhood either. She had been
repeatedly raped by her mother's boyfriends from a very young age.

Chisimdi begged Ariella to wear women's clothing only at
home. She could live a safe life if she was discreet and cautious. All
she had to do was to keep her gender identity hidden. But Ariella
felt uncomfortable living as a man. Dressing like one for the rest of
her life was no longer an option for her.

Ariella wondered what would happen if she fled Nigeria, perhaps
to Europe. She felt she might have more protection there. She
had heard about people, north of where they were living, fleeing
Nigeria, and entering Italy as refugees.

Ariella decided to pack up her things and head north. Nigeria
had been experiencing violence from Boko Haram terrorists. Many
people in the north had been displaced from their homes and were

starving. Ariella, from a Christian family, was convinced she could join others from Nigeria seeking political asylum. She packed her belongings, and all the money she had managed to save and said a teary goodbye to Chisimdi and the girls. They had become her family.

In the north end of my country, I find the situation hopeless. People have no food, no money. Nowhere to live. I see no one helping. I know I must get to the coast of Libya. I walk for three weeks. I am so very tired, but still I walk. Sometimes I get a truck ride for free, but mostly walk. I sleep very little. One eye always open. I eat when I can. I keep money hidden. I know I will need later. I walk through the war zone. I am not afraid. I am more afraid to live as a man.

The situation on the Libyan coast, grave. So many people are sick. Families camping on the beach. They wait for help. All their homes are destroyed. Not many from Nigeria. Most from Libya, Tunisia. They try to escape rebellions in their country.

Many of the boats Ariella saw on the Libyan shore were old fishing boats that did not appear seaworthy. She heard stories of people dying on these boats. She heard of others, often children, flying off and drowning, of entire boats capsizing. Ariella completely understood why they boarded these boats despite the danger. It was worth taking the risk to be free.

There were humanitarian organizations on the shoreline trying to provide relief and assistance. But there were not nearly enough workers for the hundreds of displaced people, some gravely ill. Ariella was told that the wait for a safe boat to take people away from Libya was months.

Human smugglers walked around the shoreline trying to sell the people boat transportation to Europe. Their prices varied widely, as did the quality of their boats. Sometimes people paid money, but there was no boat. Ariella paid good money so that she could leave quickly. She remained on the beach in Libya only three days before setting sail.

> The boat is small and the waves large. At least it is a boat. Some boats I see leaving are rubber rafts stuffed with people. They have no real seats, nothing to lean on. I think they will never make it. My boat is sturdier.
>
> We are about sixty people. Mostly men. No children. Only a few women. We have life jackets. There is no food, no water to drink. Some men vomit from the up and down of waves. I think it will take a week to get to Italy. But we are on the boat only about fourteen hours.

By luck, or possibly grace of some god, Ariella's boat managed to cross a section of the Mediterranean. However, they did not land in Sicily, or mainland Italy. They arrived at the Italian Island of Lampedusa, which according to Ariella was about 300 km from where they left.

Before reaching land, they were spotted by humanitarian search and rescue workers. By the time Ariella's boat hit the shore, there were workers waiting for them. A few of the men aboard her boat fled. A few remained on the Island. Ariella had no idea why and she didn't ask. She remained with the majority of the group. She figured that was her only hope of getting real assistance.

They were led to a much larger, safer boat where they were greeted kindly. Someone took their lifejackets. They were asked to stand in a long line and officials recorded their name, date of birth, and country of origin. They were also asked if they were travelling alone or in a group. Once their paperwork was completed, they were given a blanket and change of clothes, and sent to board the boat. By the time Ariella stepped into the boat, there were quite a few other people already on board.

We are wet, hungry. When all lines are done, they ask us to find a spot to sit. They separate men and women. I hesitate but go with men. I don't want to draw attention to myself. I look like a young man. They will not understand. When we sit, they bring us food to eat. I did not eat soft bread since leaving Chisimdi's house more than one month ago. I chew very slowly. I do not know when there will be food again.

This second boat sailed quickly compared to the first one, and it landed in mainland Italy. Once they were safely docked, everyone was transferred to reception centres run by the Italian government. There was apparently a myriad of people there. Ariella remembers seeing police and coast guards, as well as persons who worked for immigration services.

The first station Ariella entered was a medical one. There were nurses examining people and providing first aid treatment and assistance for anyone who needed it. Those that were too ill to withstand questioning were removed and possibly taken elsewhere. Ariella doesn't know what happened to them. And she didn't want to ask. It wasn't her business.

The nurse that initially examined Ariella called for a doctor. Ariella was asked to wait in a different line. She had never seen a doctor before, and she was petrified. The doctor spent a great deal of time examining her numerous scars. Some were from the whippings she had received as a child. Others from abuse on the streets. He asked her if she had ever had any broken bones. Ariella answered she didn't know. Because she didn't.

Ariella was petrified to answer the questions honestly. She was worried that if she gave the wrong answer, they would send her back. She didn't know what to do. The doctor asked Ariella how many times she had been raped and whether she was a homosexual. Ariella was silent. She was certain they were going to put her on a boat back to Libya. She was literally shaking.

The doctor says not to be afraid. He says most migrants want to escape being poor and hungry. It will be difficult for them to stay here. Others will remain for a very long time, maybe years before processed. They might get to stay if they are being killed in home country because of their religion. They have temporary accommodation centers here. He tells about government special protections. Mostly for orphan children and victims of torture, sex violence. He knows homosexuals can be killed if they remain in African countries. I understand now. He has kind eyes. He is not judging. He is helping.

I am taken to a place with immigration officials. I feel them stare as I walk in the room. I have felt this before. I see their faces. Their eyes snigger at me walking, how I hold my arms. I try hard not to look afraid. I am too tired to change the way I move.

When I think about all this now, and when I tell my story to you, I believe the way I move, like a girl, saved my life.

The immigration officers did not ask Ariella many questions. They had the medical documentation from the doctor, which confirmed serious physical and sexual abuse. She told the authorities that she had been living on the streets of Nigeria since the age of thirteen because she liked boys. They assumed, just like her mother a few long years back, that she was a young homosexual man.

Obviously, they believed that her claim for asylum was legitimate because she was placed in line for "SPRAR," which I learned later means Sistema di Protezione per Richiedenti Asilo e Rifugiati. This is apparently a protection system for asylum seekers and refugees. Essentially, after a time, Ariella could possibly be settled in Italy and would not be forced to return to Nigeria or Libya.

However, the UNHCR working with the government determined that it might be safer for Ariella to be processed for resettlement, so that she could be transferred from Italy to either Australia or Canada for permanent residency. At that time, both countries were considered by them to be more desirable than Italy for someone like Ariella.

While Ariella was waiting for resettlement outside of Italy, she was placed within a government accommodation centre, which she described as feeling somewhat like a prison. Here the men and women were separated, and Ariella was placed with the men. It was very crowded, and the facility was not always clean. There were very few showers and toilets for the large number of men using them. The showers were open, and Ariella was very uncomfortable that men could see her body. As well, they slept with ten or twelve men in very close quarters within the same room. Food was adequate but tasteless.

Although they were permitted to leave the centre during the day, they had to return every evening by a specific time. Ariella didn't really have anywhere to go, and she didn't know anyone in Italy. Ariella emphasizes that she doesn't want to seem ungrateful for the care she received. For her, the forced accommodation with men was extremely stressful and isolating.

If you are a woman, imagine being required to live with men housed in very close quarters. Picture being forced to shower in the open and to change in front of them. Ariella was completely uncomfortable staying there, and she did not feel safe.

Ariella explains that the paperwork was very complex, as was the process. Workers with UNHCR provided her with a tremendous amount of support, and she does not believe that she could have navigated through the system without their assistance. After almost four months, Ariella's paperwork was finalized and approved. To Ariella, four months seemed like years, but she found out much later from others that her wait was actually very short in comparison.

Ariella entered Toronto when she was twenty years old.

Like others I have interviewed, the adjustment to life in Toronto has not been easy. Since coming to Canada, Ariella has struggled with PTSD. She must somehow find a way to cope with the memories and feelings of the physical and emotional trauma and abuse that she endured for most of her life.

Some days are hard. I cannot get up. I hear little girls screaming. The sound of horsewhip. I feel pain from beatings. From rape. I want to stay in bed. I talk to a special counsellor who says I should speak of the pain to heal. I want to heal. But sometimes, sometimes it is harder than the street.

Finding employment has been particularly challenging for Ariella. In her opinion, the greatest impediment to finding work has been her lack of formal education. Ariella has been studying to take her General Education Diploma (GED). If she passes the test, then she earns an Ontario High School Equivalency Certificate. However, sometimes Ariella struggles to focus, which she has been told is related to her PTSD. She does not learn as quickly as she would like, and this frustrates her greatly.

Furthermore, accessing the education she requires has also proven to be difficult. Ariella never had the opportunity to attend much schooling in Nigeria, so she needed to complete several high school courses before she was ready for the GED. Although the Ministry of Education funds Ontario's Independent Learning Centre to administer the GED, there are still costs involved. She told me that high school courses run about $40 each, and the price to register to sit and write the GED is around $100. For Ariella, this is a great deal of money.

Ariella did well in the language arts of reading and writing, but required upgrading for math, science, and social studies. She was working hard, but she had limited time during the day to study, and there were also cultural barriers for people like Ariella that made test-taking challenging.

Ariella has come to love the city of Toronto, and for the most part, people she has encountered have interacted with her in a positive manner. But sadly, not everyone here is supportive of people who are transgender. Even though cruel comments are few and far between, Ariella says that when they come, they hurt as much as a horsewhip.

Not all people are kind. A few hateful and mean ones. I will
show these people they are wrong. I tell myself I want more.
I deserve more. Over and over, I say it.

Dealing with the process of transitioning her body to affirm her gender identity has been challenging, but exciting. Ariella is grateful that she can live as herself here. She never dresses like a man. She is a woman and strives to be accepted as one. She is now quite connected with other transgender women, in particular trans women who are Black that share similar obstacles.

It is not so easy. I know some trans women do sex work. I have done sex work. It is tough to find good jobs, or any jobs. But here I am a woman. I am mostly safe. I will not stop trying.

Quite disturbing to me, Ariella told me that she has been stopped by police more than once and questioned about whether she is soliciting clients for prostitution when she was simply walking to her neighbourhood grocery store. The intersectionality of being both Black and transgender puts her at risk for harassment by police, despite all of Canada's efforts and movement forward to defend and ensure political and civil rights and freedoms.

Given everything that Ariella has endured, she still makes it clear that she doesn't want anyone's sympathy. What she needs is access to education, safe housing, employment, and high-quality health care specifically geared towards people who are transgender.

Ariella has been able to regain contact with Chisimdi, who she refers to as her sister. They communicate regularly using computers at the public library. Ariella was initially quite surprised that nobody vandalized or stole these computers, and that she was able to use them for free. Although not the case everywhere in Nigeria, the area where Ariella is from had no libraries and no access to free computers, or any computers.

Once Ariella earns her GED, she would like to go to college for hairdressing or aesthetics. She has been passionate about this kind of work since acting as a personal assistant to Chisimdi and the girls when she was a teenager, struggling to understand her identity. She thinks it would be wonderful to "make women feel beautiful, as princesses."

Like everyone that I interviewed, Ariella did not want her real name used in her story. But she could not think of an appropriate pseudonym, so she told me I could select any name for her that was fitting of a princess. I picked the name Ariel.

In the 1989 animated Disney movie *The Little Mermaid*, Ariel is the quintessential princess, with her long flowing hair, fluttery eyelashes, and a gentle voice. Her femaleness is not in any way defined by what is below her waist. Ariella had never seen this movie, but after watching it, she loved that I had named her after such a magnificent princess. However, she felt that the name Ariel was too plain and that the name Ariella was much more majestic. This is how the name Ariella came to be.

Ariella would like everyone to know that *Princess* Ariella is alive and well and living in Toronto. Since initially interviewing her, I have learned that she has earned her GED. I occasionally bump into her in downtown Toronto. Sometimes she acknowledges me, sometimes she doesn't. I take the lead from her. Maybe because I know her story, I remind her of the past.

I want to acknowledge the significant time Ariella spent with me so that I could accurately portray her life and her journey to Toronto. The atrocities she has endured, beginning when she was a young child, are incomprehensible. The entire time I was writing about her life it felt unreal, like I was describing the plot of some deeply disturbing movie; a movie that I couldn't stop, and I couldn't rewind. It is a testament to Ariella's unbelievable strength of character that she never lost hope. As far as I am concerned, with all due respect to Ariella, she isn't a princess. She is a superhero. For more detailed information on being transgender, please refer to Jamie Raines's book, *The T in LGBT: Everything you need to know about being trans.*[19]

#

I wish I could report that the situation for people with non-conventional sexual orientations and gender identities has improved across Nigeria since Ariella left the country. Sadly, this is not the case. In fact, in many areas, things would appear to be even worse. Same-sex relations continue to be against the law across the country, and secular law can punish men with a sentence of up to fourteen years in jail for being found guilty of the crime of being homosexual. Sharia law makes this crime punishable by death, and ten Nigerian states, which are mostly in the north, practice Sharia law. The Criminal Code in Nigeria does not directly address sex acts between women, but it is criminalized because the word "person" is used in the Criminal Code when it refers to any of the same-sex offenses that are described. 2SLGBTQ+ people are not even permitted to socialize in a group together.

In 2014, long before Ariella came to Canada, the Same-Sex Marriage Prohibition Act (SSMPA) became law in Nigeria.[20] Although the identified purpose of this law was to prohibit marriage of same-sex couples, the implications of the law went far beyond same-sex marriage to include any same-sex activity, including affectionate touches, which could put gay couples in jail for up to ten years.

Further, the act stated that membership in any group, club, or organization that had any relationship with homosexuality, even agencies providing information or assistance to people living with HIV/AIDS, could mean a prison sentence of ten years. This meant that assisting a person who is homosexual was a punishable offense, making it difficult, if not impossible, for people who are gay or transgender to access medical or any other assistance they required. It also effectively stripped 2SLGBTQ+ people of the ability to file complaints or take any legal action. By 2021, the situation initially created in 2014 had not improved. Even the mere discussion of LGBTQ rights was criminalized.

April 2022 saw a proposed amendment to the SSMPA that would make what they termed "cross-dressing" illegal and punishable by time in jail. There could also be an exorbitant fine that most people would be unable to afford. People in Nigeria are not permitted to wear clothing that does not match their perceived gender. Queer activists in 2022 reported that Nigerians were not yet having conversations about the concept of gender as a social construct, and that the term non-binary had yet to make it into mainstream culture as it has become in the West.

As of 2023, Nigerian law has remained the same, so in this regard, things have not really changed since Ariella lived there. There have apparently been rising incidents of mob violence in Nigeria with the primary purpose of physically harming people based on their sexual orientation or gender identity. Some of the victims of this abuse are not even homosexual. However, if these mobs perceive individuals as gay or gender non-conforming due to stereotypes or implicit bias, they become potential targets for hate crimes.

It is important to note that the SSMPA is neither consistent with nor in compliance with Nigeria's Constitution, which promotes dignity for all people and prohibits torture. Human rights groups from within Nigeria as well as international human rights activists have all opposed the SSMPA. But this does not appear to have had a significant impact on the situation. Many areas of Nigeria are clearly not safe for people who have a non-conventional sexual orientation, gender identity, or gender expression.

The abuse and mistreatment of people who are 2SLGBTQ+ appears to be intertwined with culture and religion in Nigeria, where ultra-conservative Christians and Muslims reside. One thing many members of these religious groups seem to share is a common hatred of homosexuals, and they view it as their religious responsibility to punish them or completely remove them from society where at all possible. Islamic extremists have attacked humanitarian and first aid workers as well as hospital and government officials who provided service and care to 2SLGBTQ+ people.

Boko Haram continues to rampage Nigeria, particularly in the north. This group rejects Western teachings and beliefs and is attempting to instate and enforce Sharia law. Many people are forced to vacate their homes quickly when Boko Haram attacks their villages, so they are left with nothing. Camps for internally displaced persons are lacking in proper sanitation (reportedly up to 100 people may share one toilet) and safe drinking water is scarce. *The Global Displacement Tracking Report 41* from June 2022 reported that between February 14 and March 30, 2022, there were over two million Internally Displaced Persons in Nigeria, with the states of Adamawa, Bauchi, Borno, Gombe, Taraba, and Yobe being the most impacted.[21]

In June 2021, the death of the Boko Haram leader Abubakar Shekau was reported in the media. This apparently hasn't stopped the violence, and the world seems to be aware that Boko Haram has most likely committed war crimes against humanity.

There is other reported violence in both the northeast and northwest areas of the country. The *2022 Human Rights Watch Report* identified that in 2021, more than one thousand children were kidnapped by bandits in the northwest of the country.[22] Protesters of this and other atrocities have been met with police brutality and other acts of violence.

Some areas of Nigeria that are not under attack are ravished with extreme poverty, and living conditions in these parts of the country can be horrific. Sometimes families are unable to feed all their children, so the older ones are forced to the streets. This is not an act of cruelty; it is a question of survival. To exacerbate this situation, Nigeria has suffered from the aftermath of floods and storms, further depleting already limited resources. The COVID pandemic greatly impacted Nigeria, dramatically increasing the number of people that were food compromised. The country does not have a reliable or consistent social net to protect people. 2SLGBTQ+ people are not the only people who are suffering here, but they are certainly among the most vulnerable.

Nigeria continues to battle its HIV epidemic. Many of the people living with HIV on the streets in Nigeria also have tuberculosis. Children in poverty are often left to fend for themselves when adults in their lives abandon them, die, or are too sick to provide care for them.

In 2021, a ban on X (formerly known as Twitter) in Nigeria happened, which further reduced people's ability to share accurate information to assist those suffering, in danger, or at risk of not getting the help they need. Nigeria, like numerous other countries, has suffered from years of corruption as well as political unrest, and there has been little, if any, funding for basic services such as medical care. It was disturbing to learn that Ariella had never even seen a doctor until she was examined by one in Italy as a person seeking asylum. Ariella probably required emergency medical attention many times during her life, especially after enduring horrifying rapes on the street, or when Chisimdi found her barely alive in a laneway. Who knows how many times her broken bones were left to heal on their own? Access to basic health care is one of the very serious issues facing people in numerous areas in Nigeria, regardless of their sexual orientation or gender identity.

While the situation for 2SLGBTQ+ people living in Nigeria can be perilous, they are clearly not the only ones there fighting for their lives. Living conditions for many people without privilege are grim. At this moment in history, there is not a feel-good story for 2SLGBTQ+ people in Nigeria.

Nigeria isn't the only country in Africa where 2SLGBTQ+ people are at significant risk. At least half of the countries in the world where it is a criminal offense to participate in sexual activity with someone of the same sex are in Africa, and four of the countries where it is punishable by death are situated on this continent.[23] Most African countries are intolerant of people who are 2SLBTQ+. In countries such as Uganda, acts of cruelty are rampant against people who have non-conventional orientations or gender identities. There, lesbian, gay, bisexual, transsexual, and intersexed people experience numerous human rights violations, including denial of health care, loss of employment, eviction from their homes, and baseless arrests, as well as abuse and extortion by police. Of the fifty-four countries in Africa, South Africa is the only country that has legalized same-sex marriage.[24]

Ariella's story is unique to her, but she is also representative of trans women around the world, in particular trans women of colour, who are frequently targets for murder. The Trans Murder Monitoring project (TMM), which began in 2009, collects reports of murders of gender diverse and transgender people worldwide. It is important to keep in mind that they can only report on the murders globally where it was specified that the person was transgender or gender diverse. As well, it is quite likely that most of these murders go unreported or they are misreported.

According to a recent TMM report, between October 1, 2021, and September 30, 2022, ninety-five percent of those murdered were trans women or trans feminine people.[6] As well, even though race or ethnicity of the victims was not always specified, when it was, over sixty-five percent of the time, the person murdered was Black, Brown, or a member of another racialized group. Latin America and the Caribbean were the world regions that reported the highest number of these killings. The Human Rights Campaign is a large American organization that tracks the murders of people in the

United States. In 2022, they reported that eighty-three percent of the transgender people murdered there were people of colour, with fifty-four percent being Black transgender women.[25]

Before meeting Ariella, I had no idea just how extreme the abuse to 2SLGBTQ+ could be in some countries and I am guessing you probably didn't know either. But now you do. There is no turning back.

Transgender rights are human rights.

Ziad and Mazn:
A Love Story

How Ziad and Mazn came to be interviewed for this book is quite fortuitous. My wife and I were attending a 2SLGBTQ+ film night at a local university and Ziad was there with a male colleague of mine who is gay. Introductions were made. My wife was able to communicate with Ziad easily because they are both fluent in Arabic. We learned that Ziad had come to Canada as a refugee from Syria with his partner Mazn (who was not with him at the time) because of their sexual orientation. My wife, who is the antithesis of shy, shamelessly volunteered the information that I had begun writing a book about exactly that, and the rest, as they say is history.

Ziad and Mazn were both born and raised in Syria, but they grew up in very different environments and had very different beginnings. They arrived in Toronto as refugees one year before I interviewed them, well-educated and full of expectations for a safer and more authentic life. Their journey to Canada was long and onerous. They existed in Malaysia in what Ziad referred to as "frozen time" for more than three years, waiting for their paperwork to be processed. Canada was never on their radar for their new home because United States, Australia, and New Zealand were the three countries offered to them by the UNHCR. They did not learn they would be coming to Canada until their final interview with the refugee board, and even then, they were told they would be going to Montreal, a large Canadian city in the province of Quebec. Ziad and Mazn never had a specific end location in mind. Their goal was to find a place where they could live safely together as a couple. But more on that later.

I interviewed Ziad and Mazn individually, on different occasions. Communication was free and open, but at times challenging. They spoke to me in English, a language that did not yet come effortlessly to them. At the time of their interviews, Mazn was more comfortable than Ziad communicating in English, mostly because he said his father pressured him to speak English when he was younger. I was astounded by their willingness to speak to me about the intimate details of their life.

Ziad is the oldest of four children. He was raised in a Druze family in a large city in Syria. Like many religions, the Druze faith, which follows a book called The Epistles of Wisdom or Rasa'il al-Hikma, does not accept homosexuality. Religion and culture are often intimately tied, but Ziad feels that for his family, the pull of the culture is stronger than that of his religion. He is quick to point out that the Druze women do not typically cover their heads in the same way as women who are Muslim. I am not entirely sure why, but this was an important distinction that Ziad wanted to ensure that I understood.

Ziad remembers experiencing feelings for men when he was around thirteen. However, he thought that what he was feeling was all in his mind, and somehow not real. Growing up in Syria, homosexuality was not something that was ever openly discussed, and it was rarely mentioned. Ziad believed the stereotype he had heard that men who were homosexual were all very feminine, dressed in girl's clothing, and wore lipstick. He did not in any way identify with any of those behaviours, so it was easy for him to convince himself that he wasn't homosexual. Since he was unaware of the existence of any other boys or men who had sexual attraction for the same gender, he kept these feelings to himself. He described his extended family and his friends to me as "super straight" on multiple occasions. I don't think this means he believes there are degrees of straightness. Moreso, I think he was emphasizing that the people in his life were both conventional and conservative in their sexual orientation as well as their beliefs about sexuality.

While Ziad's father was alive, he knew he would be unable to think about his sexual attractions and what that might mean. It would have been considered completely unacceptable for him to speak about these feelings both culturally as well as given his family's beliefs. He certainly would not have been able to act on them. Consequently, Ziad did the prescribed thing, dating girls and having girlfriends so that he would not draw any suspicion to himself. But in his words, "I live in prison inside."

Sadly, when Ziad was around twenty-three years of age, his father passed away. It was expected for him to become the man of the household and support his family, a role he assumed freely, without hesitation. This seems like a huge burden for such a young man to be responsible for an entire family, but Ziad is extremely devoted to them, especially his mother. Ziad explains that like many other women in his culture, Ziad's mother did not complete high school. Studying was not considered necessary for women, at least at that time. She has always believed that her duty for life is the care of her husband and children, and role which is revered by her culture. Further, it was understood that she would never remarry should something happen to her spouse.

Consequently, when her husband died, she was unaware of how to deal with issues outside of her home. Ziad explains that she did not even know how to do the grocery shopping or manage finances of any kind which left him with the tremendous responsibility of taking care of the entire household, and everyone living in it. He does point out that the culture in his country has been changing, and women are becoming more educated and entering into the work force in greater numbers.

As a young man, Ziad found himself juggling many different life events. He was taking care of his family, completing university, and fulfilling his obligation to military service all around the same time. In Syria, all young men must do military service for one-and-a-half years when they turn eighteen years of age, or once they have completed university. Ziad considers himself extremely lucky because his tenure in the military finished just fifteen days before the civil war erupted.

While in the military, Ziad was dating one woman exclusively and he promised her that they would marry after his service was completed. He describes this woman as being "really lovely" and deserving of a good life. Ziad cared deeply about her, and he did not want to see her get hurt. Since he knew deep inside that he would never go through with the wedding because of his sexual orientation, he fabricated an excuse and broke off the engagement.

Ziad took some time to reflect on this, saying that she was completely devastated because she was certain he was the love of her life. However, he believes that he did the right and moral thing, not "dragging her into the closet" along with him. He feels very strongly that it would have been crueller to have married her knowing that he would never love her in the manner that she deserved, then to have broken her heart. He believed, or maybe hoped, that time would heal the emotional pain of losing what she thought was going to be her life partner.

Upon graduation from university, Ziad explains that he was still very "straight acting." He was also extremely busy taking care of his family and trying to build their equity, so that they would have a secure future. To increase the family assets, Ziad began purchasing and renovating apartments, and then reselling them. Consequently, he did not really have any time to focus on himself, his needs, or his sexual orientation. Ziad told me that his family shows him great respect because he took care of them for so long. He believes that if his mother knew he was gay, she would still love him, but would not disclose this information to her extended family or any of her friends. Ziad told me that his mother did meet Mazn, but he was introduced as a good friend, not a romantic partner. On this point I can relate. My wife's family thinks we are best friends. Which I suppose is true, but they do not understand the depth of our relationship or the commitment we have to each other as life partners.

On top of everything Ziad was juggling, he had an excellent career with an agency that is affiliated with the government. He holds a master's degree in a professional field and his work reflected his educational achievement. To ensure his confidentiality, Ziad requested that I not report his actual place of work or even the nature of it.

Up until now in his story, Ziad didn't know any other gay men and he was completely unaware that there was a community of gay men in Syria. This all changed when he met someone on Facebook who gave him information about gay websites and dating apps. He believes he was around twenty-seven or twenty-eight when he made this life-changing discovery. Looking at this through a privileged, Westernized lens, it is difficult to appreciate how someone could be almost thirty years of age and not ever have met anyone who was gay. But quite likely, Ziad is not unique in his experience. This reality speaks volumes about the oppression of people who are gay in a fiercely homophobic country. The odds are that he had met people who are gay previously, but he wouldn't have known that they were not heterosexual because everyone was closeted.

When Ziad decided to venture out and create his first profile on a meet-up app for homosexual men, he was concerned about protecting his identity from his family and co-workers. He was also very cautious for his own safety. In his words, he was "super scared." Gay men in Syria were being subjected to persecution, torture, and even death. As well, Ziad had heard about police posing as gay men on websites to entrap men who were homosexual. Understandably, he did not post his picture on the site, nor did he provide any identifying information about his physical attributes. Ziad really wanted to meet other gay men, but he was petrified of being outed.

To make the situation even worse, it was becoming increasingly difficult for Ziad to continue to live in Syria for many other reasons. Given his country's horrific treatment of homosexual people, especially gay men, he would never have an opportunity to live his life with another man. But even if he was willing to sacrifice never living in an "out" relationship, it was beginning to appear strange to people that Ziad was unmarried. He wasn't at all trying to brag, but he explained that he is essentially, a good-looking man with an excellent job, a house, and a car. In his culture, it would be totally incongruent for a man of his stature to remain unmarried. He would be considered a "catch" by single women and their families, and as he says, "he would have his selection of women to marry." Many families would be approaching his mother to see if their daughter might be a suitable partner for him.

Ziad's mother was having increasing difficulty struggling to understand why her eldest child wasn't getting married as he was getting older. She emphasized to him that she really wanted to be given at least one child from him. She was repeatedly bemoaning to Ziad that she needed a grandchild to bring her great happiness before she died. In a very real way, Ziad was trapped, even though it wasn't a physical confinement.

Mazn is ten years younger than Ziad, and I learned that he had a very different upbringing. The day I interviewed Mazn was the first time we had ever met. We met in a mid-town coffee shop. I arrived first, but I somehow knew who he was the moment he walked in. He greeted me with his dazzling smile, and such openness and trust that it was overwhelming. Unlike Ziad, Mazn grew up in a small Christian town in Syria where people who lived there tended to remain there forever. "Lifers," as Mazn referred to them, and they all knew each other. Geographically, his town is very close to the larger city of Hama, which is predominately Muslim. This religious difference between the two places provoked a great deal of conflict among the people in his community and had a tremendous impact on Mazn when he was growing up: "We have our own limits and rules. But we are very affected by being close to Muslim cities."

Mazn elaborates that in his hometown, women dress how they please, and wear whatever they want, including short skirts and more revealing articles of clothing. But when they travel to Hama, they know that they must dress modestly if they do not want to draw attention to themselves or provoke controversy. They don't necessarily have to cover their heads, but they need to be conservative in appearance.

Mazn grew up in fear of people learning that he is Christian. His assessment is that people in Hama are very closed-minded and completely unaware of different religious perspectives. The belief of those who live in the larger cities around him is that following their Muslim faith is the only acceptable way to live. While he does not think he would be killed for being Christian, he believes there is immediate dislike. Mazn contrasts Hama with the capital city of Damascus, where some women wear their hair out, use makeup and wear modern clothing. The suburbs are not as free or accepting.

Unlike Ziad, who is the oldest in his family, Mazn is the youngest. He grew up with five sisters, and in his words, "I grew up like a girl." This suited him just fine. He was interested in playing and being with girls all the time. He enjoyed dancing, and he loved dressing up in his sisters' clothes. His real passion was art and creating things, but these interests were not deemed masculine enough in his culture. Mazn said that he faced many struggles as a child. People thought he walked and talked like a girl, and they labelled him as a sissy. In his experience, people in his country were not very accepting of gender non-conforming boys. Mazn's father made it clear that he was not very happy because he wanted his son to be man, and his belief was that the idea of a man involved in art was "nonsense."

In his father's view, art is not a respectable career for a male. His father's emphasis appeared to be on gender; on judgements about behaviours that are appropriate for males compared to those that are appropriate to females, as opposed to concerns regarding his sexual orientation. Mazn was unaware as a young child that there was "such a thing called gay." He was, however, made acutely aware of prescribed gender roles.

Mazn always loved acting, and he began performing at school and at church from a young age. He participated multiple times in his church Christmas play. As well, he enjoyed creating and making his own costumes, in addition to singing, dancing, and acting. Mazn thinks that singing some of the many songs he memorized facilitated his learning of English. Even though his father was not supportive of him engaging in the performing arts, Mazn remembers that his father was impressed with one Syrian entertainer because he was well-educated and could speak English. His father always preached to Mazn that he needed to learn to speak English if he was determined to pursue a career in acting. Mazn continued acting until high school. When he joined the drama club, he found that the other students were not that serious about the art form, which was a huge disappointment for him.

Despite his family's religion, Mazn attended an all-boys high school in Hama with a business focus. Only schools for all-girls offered fine arts programs. The teachers at his school kept badgering Mazn to change the way he looked, because they felt that he dressed like a girl. Whenever he wore a suit, or dressed in a more stereotypically male manner, he received much praise from everyone. The push for him to be gender-conforming was strong, constant, and clearly apparent.

Mazn disclosed that he met other boys his age that approached him to have sex, but he was too afraid, and he never acted on it. He felt that it would be too easy for people to find out. He also said, "my father is not blind." Some of the boys at his school tried to touch him or flirt with him, as if he was a girl. They often joked around with him or taunted him about being female. One boy repeatedly teased him and asked for kisses. He questioned Mazn about whether he was afraid and according to Mazn, this young man "took out his package" right in front of everyone. By this point, everyone was laughing at Mazn, circling around him, and taunting him. I would like to point out that it seems ironic to me that the boys were laughing at Mazn. He wasn't the one standing there with his genitals hanging out in full view of everyone.

Although Mazn's account was that the other boys were continually teasing him, in my opinion, their behaviour extended far beyond teasing. He was being bullied as well as sexually harassed, and their behaviours were cruel. Mazn felt that some of the boys who were teasing him were probably gay themselves and were also deep in the closet. Bullying him was a way to draw attention away from themselves. He said he had private conversations with a few boys who admitted they were homosexuals when they were alone, but in public they made fun of Mazn and made jokes about his feminine characteristics. Mazn reasoned that most likely, it was easier for these boys to hide their sexuality because they did not fit the stereotype of the feminine, or flamboyant gay male. He feels he is more feminine in presentation, but his perspective is that he does not do this purposefully, it's simply who he is as a person. And he has been this way since early childhood.

As Mazn matured, he received conflicting messages about his love of art and interior design. On the one hand, he was being told that these were not interests appropriate for a male to pursue. On the other hand, by the time he was fourteen and fifteen years of age, people were purchasing lamps, candles, and other things that he had crafted, and they were seeking him out for assistance with their Christmas decorations. His handmade crafts were admired by many who told him they loved his work, and yet, because he was a male, it was also stigmatized by others who could not open their mind beyond their rigid binary construction of gender.

Mazn could not envision a future for himself in Syria. He had spent his entire younger life creating handmade things and doing interior design for others. Although his mother supported his aspiration to be an interior designer, his father did not, and insisted that Mazn not pursue anything involving fine arts at the post-secondary level. Mazn heard the view repeatedly that this was a profession for females only. He had essentially been ridiculed for being himself his entire life not just by people in his community, but by his own father.

When Mazn enrolled in university, he studied business during the first semester at his father's request, but his grades were not that good. Once he went against his father's belief that this area of study was for females only, and changed his major to interior design, he began earning all "A" grades. While attending university, Mazn met another gay student, who was more open to having conversations with him and to answering any of his questions. The two of them began texting, and this friend introduced him to his social circle, which included other gay males. Three of Mazn's sisters were also away from home while he was attending university. One was in acting school, one was a dancer in a troupe, and the third was studying nursing. Clearly, he is from a very artistically talented family!

Mazn moved to Damascus around the same time that his one sister was pursuing acting. Since his sister was in the dramatic arts, she had been exposed to people who are gay and was aware they existed. Mazn hypothesized that people in the arts tended to be more open to various types of people. Unfortunately, Mazn was disappointed to learn that his sister would not become an ally to him, and she made it known that she did not want to see him interacting with any gay people.

While attending university, there was one street that was known to be a hangout for men who were more feminine than masculine in presentation. According to him, it was not uncommon for men who regularly dressed very manly to alter the way they dressed when they were visiting the "sissy street." Mazn disclosed to his sister that he had met people in that location, and she had even accompanied him there on occasion. However, as soon as she saw him interacting with boys who were feminine acting, or those who were known to be gay, she requested that he stop mingling with them. Whenever she saw him with a group of gay men, she would ignore him and pretend that she didn't know him. Although he did not explicitly say so, it must have been painful for him to have his personhood erased by his own sister. Mazn is very expressive when he speaks, and I could see the pain on his face when he described his sister's behaviour towards him.

Mazn described himself as a tiny man, and quite feminine in presentation. I did not view him as tiny, as much as petite or having a small frame. I would agree that his gestures and movements would not be considered gender-conforming for males, if one had a narrow view of gender expression. And the way someone moves doesn't necessarily make them gay. Despite this, Mazn believed that there were some areas in Syria where he would be at risk for being murdered for being too feminine and/or too gay. He noted that even from street to street within the same city, there were differences in the way feminine men were treated. But he emphasized that it was not safe in Syria for gay men or feminine looking or acting men regardless of their sexual orientation.

Mazn did retain his passion for acting for a very long time, but he does not believe that he would ever have a future career in this profession, even at an international level, because he does not fit the media portrayal of Middle Eastern men as "fit and masculine." Essentially, movies either portray them as exotic and carnal, or cast them as evil terrorists. Neither of these stereotypically representations has any appeal to Mazn.

Ziad met Mazn on a meet-up website for homosexual men, and they began communicating with each other. After chatting for a time, Mazn asked Ziad for his picture. Mazn felt they had a connection, and he wanted to determine whether Ziad was handsome and his type. To this end, Mazn had already sent a picture of himself to Ziad, but it was "pretty fuzzy" and difficult to distinguish details of his face. However, Ziad was not willing to trust a stranger, so he decided to post a picture of himself from his neck down to his waist, without a shirt. Only his naked torso was visible, no face, and no bottom half. Ziad laughed when he told me that he assumes Mazn must have liked what he saw, since he agreed to meet in person. I asked Mazn what might have happened if he didn't like his face when they first met in person. Almost scandalously, Mazn waved his hand above his neck, and then below his waist to indicate that Ziad "liked this very much." This gesture was not only unexpected, but it was hilarious, to the point, and a tad risqué!

Quite a romantic and charming beginning to their relationship! After Mazn approved of Ziad's torso picture, the two men first met in person at a coffee shop. Both agreed that Ziad arrived late, because the army was blocking the streets, and he couldn't get through. When he finally appeared, and saw Mazn sitting in the coffee shop, he thought he appeared so young that he literally checked his identification to ensure that he was of legal age. Not that it is relevant, but both Mazn and Ziad are extremely beautiful looking men. Despite the ten-year age difference, their age gap doesn't appear that evident when you meet them in person.

Mazn is remarkably candid about their first meeting. He commented that although he thought Ziad was very handsome, he didn't feel he was his type. Mazn prefers bigger, stronger, and highly masculine-looking men. Nevertheless, both mentioned they had a great deal of fun, flirting, and joking with each other. They felt they could become friends, but probably not romantic partners.

Friendship seems to be a great place to begin a relationship, and their romantic attraction to each other blossomed over time. But two men attempting to navigate dating in a fiercely heterosexual and homophobic society was no easy feat, aside from the obvious safety issues created by Syria being actively involved in a civil war.

Once they began dating, Ziad and Mazn could not easily go to the same places or hang out together. The area of the city where gay men frequented was very close to Ziad's place of work, and he was petrified that people would see him there. If anyone inquired about how Ziad had come to know Mazn, he would simply answer that he was attending university in the city. This was true as Mazn was in his final year of study when they met. However, there could be no suggestion of anything more intimate or personal than a casual friendship. It was not culturally acceptable and was physically dangerous for them both to do so.

A confirmation of this fact is that a friend of Ziad's had once been stopped by people pretending to be gay. They stripped him of his clothes and beat him. They also stole his phone, presumably to identify other gay men from the information in his contacts. Apparently, many people on the street walked by and observed the beating but did nothing to stop or interfere with the attack. Ziad's friend was a victim of a hate crime but there was nowhere he could go to complain or to get justice. Police were not sympathetic to homosexuals and sometimes participated in violence against men they perceived as gay.

While in Syria, Ziad and Mazn were able to walk around together and talk, but there was absolutely no opportunity for intimacy. If close friends or family members were near, they pretended they didn't know each other. When they were together, they could not even hold hands. It was a full year before they were able to engage in any kind of physical contact.

The civil war in Syria created even more hurdles for Ziad and Mazn. Travelling took inordinate amounts of time, and there were designated checkpoints for travel within the city. Ziad commented that he would get stopped multiple times just attempting to get into the downtown core. At best, it was an arduous beginning.

Despite all the challenges of being together, even just for conversation, Ziad and Mazn developed deep feelings for each other. By now, Mazn had completed his university degree and was expected to return to his hometown. The two men knew remaining in Syria was not an option for them if they wanted to pursue a life together, and they began to plan how they would navigate leaving. They decided they would apply for refugee status from Malaysia, because it was the only country nearby that would permit them to enter without any kind of Visa.

Ziad was deeply committed to ensuring that his family was safe and had sufficient means to be comfortable. He has a brother who is thirteen years younger, and in his words, he is "more like a son than a brother." Unfortunately, his brother became of military age when Syria was at war. Ziad knew that once his brother was recruited into the military, he would be forced to fight and kill other Syrians. Ziad was determined to protect his brother from any direct exposure to the horrors of this war. He also feared for his brother's life. To ensure his safety, Ziad took his brother to Beirut, Lebanon. This was the very first time that Ziad had ever left Syria, and he did not know a soul in Lebanon. But he risked this trip, determined that his brother should remain safe and not be exposed to the war.

Mazn informed his parents that he wanted to pursue a graduate degree in Malaysia, so they had no reason to question why he did not want to return home. Once he arrived in Malaysia, he immediately applied to the office of the UNHCR to seek asylum and leave that part of the world. He was informed that there would likely be a one-year wait before he could get his first appointment. Since he was enrolled as a legitimate graduate student, he was granted a student visa, which permitted him to rent an apartment for one year.

Once Mazn was in graduate school, Ziad visited him. His first visit lasted a full month. The second time he wanted to return to Malaysia for a few weeks, he was only granted a nine-day visitor visa. However, some of the officials were corrupt, which worked in Ziad's favour because he purchased "under the table documentation" without going through the regular channels. This enabled him to stay in Malaysia again for an entire month. It was during these lengthy visits the two men discussed and formulated their escape plan.

Mazn and Ziad were in contact with UNHCR, but they were unable to confirm where they might be going and how long the process might take. Still, they were willing to relocate to any country in the world that would permit them to live together as a couple, and where they would be safe and free to do so.

After Ziad's second visit with Mazn, he returned to Syria. But before he could rejoin Mazn one last time and carry out their plan to leave for good, he felt it was his responsibility to ensure his mother was provided for. He bought and then sold an apartment to secure the funds he needed to obtain a suitable place for her. He wanted to ensure she would not just be safe, but comfortable. With the income he had made, he purchased her a home in the south of Syria closer to one of his sisters. He then assisted her in packing and moving all their belongings into the new place. Because Ziad's father was deceased, his mother was receiving a pension, and she also held other assets, so Ziad knew she would have the capacity to live comfortably.

When Ziad believed that his mother was secure, he resigned from his job and informed her that he was leaving Syria. Her assumption was that he was departing because of the war, and he didn't correct her. But he also didn't lie. He explained that he was leaving his home country to find a way to survive, which was absolutely the truth. Since many people were fleeing Syria for reasons not related to sexual orientation or gender identity, it didn't appear odd to Ziad's work colleagues that he was leaving. There were probably no red flags raised at that time, at least none that he was aware of.

Once Ziad left Syria, he left forever. He booked himself a flight and moved to Malaysia to join his life partner. Ziad was emotional when he told me that he missed everything about his country, but he clarified that he meant the country he knew prior to the civil war. In his heart, Syria changed after that: "the place where I lived does not exist anymore." He misses his mother most of all. He was essentially with her his entire life, for thirty-two years. "I never left her side, not even while at university."

After living in Malaysia for two or three months, the two men were contacted for a first interview with the UNHCR. Since both men were considered at risk of violence directed at them because of their sexual orientation they were given an UNHCR ID which permitted them to remain in Malaysia. Unfortunately, they were not legally allowed to work.

Approximately every nine months, Mazn and Ziad were called for interviews where they were asked often invasive and personal questions about their relationship, including specific details about their sexual relations. This continued for more than three years. What made this even more difficult was that they could be questioned about something they might have mentioned two years previously at an interview, and their answers needed to match perfectly to be considered credible. Mismatched answers could potentially be enough for their claim to be rejected. Consequently, these interviews were extraordinarily stressful. Authorities were looking to identify detailed documentation of the same-sex relationship status of the claimants. However, it can be difficult for someone living in a country where their safety and even their life depended on people not knowing their sexual orientation to have any "proof" of either sexuality or of a romantic relationship with a same-sex person. They may never have officially dated out of fear, and even if they had, they might not have any photos, texts, or other things to corroborate their story. This was the case for Mazn and Ziad. They dated in secret when they could, but they could never behave publicly as if they were on an actual date. There was essentially no concrete "proof" that they were either gay or a couple. Because Mazn fits a stereotype of how some authorities believe gay men act, he and Ziad think this somehow increased their credibility as a gay couple. While Ziad isn't overly masculine presenting, he would be considered gender-conforming in presentation by most people.

Since Ziad was stuck in suspended animation without papers entitling him to work, he secured lower paying jobs such as at fast food restaurants where he could be paid cash under the table. This was the only way they were able to survive. While Mazn was in graduate school, they had a place to live, however, once his year of studies was completed, the two men were essentially homeless. They had no idea how long they would have to exist in this manner and wrongly assumed that the process would be much quicker. They survived by couch surfing and staying with other people.

As time went on, Ziad was able to secure some work teaching engineering, for which he was paid in cash. Both men accepted any work that didn't require official papers and would pay them without a paper trail. They continued existing in this unsettling life for more than three years.

Ziad's brother came to visit him while he was in Malaysia. He feels his brother may have had a suspicion of his sexuality because at the time, he and Mazn were living in a two-bedroom apartment, but they shared the same room which had only one bed. However, this was never mentioned or discussed between the siblings. As fate would have it, during the time of his brother's visit, the two men were called for an interview. Ziad was afraid to leave his brother alone in Malaysia while they went to be interviewed so Ziad purchased him a ticket to Turkey. His brother then walked from Turkey to Hamburg, Germany, which took him about a month. Since his brother spoke English, he became a translator for other Syrian people. At the time that I interviewed these men, Ziad's brother was still working there, but he had moved on from being a translator. Even though his brother is heterosexual, he cannot return to Syria. Should he cross the border back to Syria, he will immediately be captured and forced into the military.

When it was finally time for Mazn's and Ziad's resettlement interview, they were told that Canada would likely accept them, even though it hadn't been one of the countries they were offered. They were first informed that they would be going to Montreal, Quebec, although neither of these men speak French. The UNHCR apparently assisted them throughout the application process and helped to prepare them for their final interview with the Canadian Embassy by explaining to them the interview process and the nature of the questioning they should expect. Ziad and Mazn were interviewed together as well as separately. They both expressed their gratitude that the man who conducted that last interview was both kind and nice. Mazn joked that perhaps the interviewer was himself gay.

Mazn was called in for his interview first. Ziad explained that Mazn was likely both highly dramatic and emotional during this interview, which apparently lasted only about twenty minutes. Although he reportedly didn't cry, he was apparently on the brink of tears the entire time. Existing for more than three years without a place to live, and without any legal right to work, must have been extremely gruelling. I can only imagine that being grilled about one's sexual orientation and sex life must have been agonizing. It is not surprising that Mazn, or anyone else in his position, would have been extremely emotional. I do appreciate that Mazn might have also been theatrical, speaking with great expression and an abundance of physical gestures.

The interview process lasted between three and four hours, which seemed like a lifetime. However, the two men learned later that many people have interviews that last much longer. Having to prove you are gay or transgender is not as easy as it might seem, and people in positions of making decisions about whether claims are authentic may be assessing potential refugees through a heteronormative lens with very stereotypic assumptions. And even though the staff are highly trained, they may believe that the horrific treatment and torture some of the claimants from different countries have received because of their sexual orientation or gender identity may be exaggerated or untrue.

Mazn and Ziad were informed that someone had sponsored them to enter Canada, but they were not provided with any identifying information of the sponsor. They also received assistance from the Rainbow Railroad as well as from the Canadian Government. They were not informed until they were in the final interview that they would be flying to Toronto. In the end, they travelled to Canada with two other gay men from their part of the world who were not a couple. All four of them were going to be accepted as refugees for resettlement in Toronto, Canada.

Ziad and Mazn's journey to Canada was long and onerous. Ziad misses his mother most of all, but he doesn't want to bring her to Canada because she is happy in Syria. He wonders if it might ever be possible for her to visit him. Mazn, too, can never go home again. If he does, he will be forced into the military, because unlike Ziad, Mazn never fulfilled his military conscription. He believes it might be possible to pay his way out of this obligation, but the amount of money to ensure this happened would likely be prohibitive.

As fate, or possibly lady luck, would have it, Mazn and Ziad landed in Toronto in the month of June, which happens to be Pride month. Mazn was completely amazed by this experience.

> All these people are gay! How could so many people be so gay at the same time? I had never seen anything like this in my life. Flags everywhere. Lesbians. I never really saw gay women before. This was another world.

Mazn used his talent and creativity and sewed his own costume for his first Pride parade appearance. He shared a picture with me, where he wore a metallic jumpsuit, which fit him like a glove. He marched proudly in his very first pride parade!

Ziad reported that he continues to have difficulty using the word gay. He had lived his entire life pretending to be straight and existing in the closet, and he was still feeling uncomfortable telling people about his sexual orientation.

Both men explained that they are happy because they are together, and they are safe. However, their first year had not been easy. They had high expectations for the future, but much of these were quickly squashed. They have found it very difficult to find work that is commensurate with their educational levels. They face many challenges they didn't anticipate, such as the process to have their education and qualifications acknowledged, and finding work that affords them a comfortable living. At the time of my interview with him, Ziad was trying to establish recognition of his master's degree. As well, to become a professional engineer in Ontario, he needed a P.Eng. licence from the province of Ontario. He also required one year of experience supervised by a licensed engineer. However, most positions require Canadian experience to be hired, but you cannot gain such experience unless you are first hired. The situation is the very definition of a vicious circle. While Ziad had begun the process towards getting his engineering license, it will take at least eighteen months to complete. He will be required to study again, but this time in English, and he hasn't been in university for many years. He thinks it will be difficult to return to the classroom after such a long time away from the academic environment. Recently, I've learned that Ziad and Mazn are now permanent residents of Canada.

After interviewing Ziad and Mazn, I was curious to know why they were not granted work permits when they were given papers to legally remain in Malaysia. The reason is likely related to the definition of refugee, as well as international standards for the treatment, protection, and legal rights of refugees, which were developed by the 1951 Refugee Convention and supplemented by its 1967 Protocol.[26] This was adapted by the United Nations to fulfill the 1948 Universal Declaration of Human Rights recognition that people have the right to seek asylum elsewhere if they are being persecuted in their home country. Malaysia as a country is not tied to the 1951 Convention and refugees are not recognized under the country's law. It is most likely that the UNHCR card Mazn and Ziad initially received was only for identification purposes and would not provide them with any legal status whatsoever within the country. This eventually proved problematic for them because without employment, it was difficult to secure any housing.

#

To understand the situation for people who are 2SLGBTQ+ in Syria, it is necessary to gain awareness of what life is like there. As of September 2023, Syria had been in a civil war for twelve years. According to a recent UNHCR report:

> Since 2011, more than 14 million Syrians have been forced to flee their homes in search of safety. More than 6.8 million Syrians remain internally displaced in their own country where seventy percent of the population is in need of humanitarian assistance and ninety percent of the population live below the poverty line. Approximately 5.5 million Syrian refugees live in the five countries [neighbouring] Syria— Türkiye, Lebanon, Jordan, Iraq[,] and Egypt. Germany is the largest [non-neighbouring] host country[,] with more than 850,000 Syrian refugees.[27]

Refugees from Syria are in over 130 countries around the world. Recently, Turkey and Lebanon began promoting the return of

Syrians to their home country even though it remains unsafe for them to do so.

It has been estimated that as high as seventy percent of the population of Syria needs some kind assistance, such as with health care and securing food. Water is expensive, and almost two million children are reportedly out of school. Many schools have been damaged or destroyed, and some have been taken over by the military. Children as young as seven years of age have been recruited as soldiers and high numbers of children are suffering from malnourishment.

Involvement of some other countries offering assistance has allegedly been for financial or political gain. Military troops both for and against the government are guilty of committing human rights violations and barbaric acts of violence. To add to the complexity of situation, Jihadist groups have taken advantage of the fragility of the situation. The result of this war has been devastating with hundreds of thousands of Syrians being killed and many more being displaced.

The situation for anyone living in Syria is grim, but people that identify as being 2SLGBTQ+ face additional challenges. People who are gay, in particular gay men, are sometimes murdered by their own families, and there have been reports of them being tortured and even pushed or thrown off buildings. According to the Syrian penal code (Article 520), "unnatural" sex acts are punishable by prison, with a maximum stay of three years. Unfortunately, sexual violence against 2SLGBTQ+ people is apparently rampant, with gay men, feminine men, and transgender women receiving the brunt of the brutalization. There have been reports of torture, forced disappearance, and abuse even by some Syrian officials, although these allegations can be difficult to prove.

The country of Syria, which is just east of the Mediterranean Sea, borders or is situated very close to countries such as Iraq, Jordan,

Turkey, Egypt, and Saudi Arabia. These countries are high on the list of the numerous world regions considered to be the most unsafe for people with non-conventional sexual orientations or gender identities. Some countries in the Middle East are experiencing civil or interstate war, or civil unrest, and have reportedly committed numerous human rights violations, making them hazardous for anyone residing there, not just those who are 2SLGBTQ+.

While it is positive that Mazn and Ziad were able to seek refuge elsewhere, life in Toronto has not been easy for them, and many more gay couples from that part of the world will never make it out of their countries alive.

We need to do better.

Roberto and Eric:
Dying to Be Gay

Friends often ask me how I came to meet the people that I interviewed for this book. Sometimes, as in the case of Eric and Roberto, it was happenstance. When they first arrived in Toronto seeking asylum, they were housed in a homeless shelter. At the time, a close friend of mine was volunteering with members of his church to provide support for people who were housing compromised, and he just happened to land at the same shelter where they were lodged. My friend, who is also gay, learned that they were refugees from Mexico, and had to flee from persecution because of their sexual orientation. Eventually, he shared with them that I was writing this book, and they were eager to have their stories told. I met Eric and Roberto in July and August 2023, and they were the last two people that I interviewed.

Since I had interviewed others before them, most of whom had received atrocious treatment in their home countries because of their sexual orientation or gender identity, I thought there wasn't anything they could say that would alarm me. I was wrong. Nothing could have prepared me for the utter shock I experienced when they told me their story. If I close my eyes, I can still see the anguish on their faces as they spoke. It was haunting.

I interviewed these two young men together over lunch at a restaurant in the Church-Wellesley Village. They were excited to eat at this specific restaurant, saying they had been wanting to try it, but they didn't currently have much in the way of discretionary funds for things like eating a meal outside. I was happy to treat them. It was such a small price to pay for the privilege of hearing their stories. But I was suddenly acutely aware of my own privilege. It is very easy to take something as commonplace as having lunch together in a restaurant for granted. It was a beautiful day, and we sat outside on the patio.

Eric and Roberto are Spanish speakers, but they both speak English, although Eric's English is much stronger than Roberto's. Because of this, Eric did more talking.

I started the interview by asking them when they came out of the closet.

Roberto was sixteen when he began going out with guys, but he didn't come out to his family until he was twenty-one. Since he was living in his parent's house at the time, he was told in no uncertain terms that he must follow their rules. This meant not participating in behaviours they did not deem "Christian," and homosexuality in their view was inconsistent with their beliefs. In Roberto's view, Christianity is a "witch hunt" (his words). People from the church gossip about others and judge them. They do not approve of people who do not have a conventional sexual orientation. He also believes that "churches in Mexico take advantage of the ignorance of the people" and that they are "thieves." Roberto's family told him they would not offer him any financial support if he was gay. Although not literally forced out of the family home, there really was no choice for him but to find his own living arrangements if he was going to have an authentic life. While Roberto's family does not support him emotionally or financially because of his sexual orientation, he does not believe they would ever intentionally cause him any physical harm. I didn't understand why he made that comment until later in the interview.

Eric also came out to his family when he was very young, just fifteen. His family told him that he can't be gay in his neighbourhood because people in Mexico expect men to behave like men, and according to Eric, they meant you had to be "macho and manly." They did not want to be shamed or humiliated within their community because of him. Unfortunately, the passage of time never changed their homophobic perspective that men who are gay are not real men.

Over time, things appeared to escalate. When he was older, Eric became a gay-rights activist. He protested the government because even though discrimination against people with non-conventional sexual orientations or gender identities and expressions in Mexico was illegal, people with these identities were not being afforded the same access to health care, especially when it came to sexually transmitted diseases and hepatitis. As well, he was lobbying for treatment and care for people who were living with HIV/AIDS, as this was neither readily available nor easily accessible. Because of his advocacy work, Eric's family told him that he was not worthy of the family's last name. They also said they were not proud of having an openly gay son. Eric's family appeared to become increasingly antagonistic towards him over time. By now, Eric had become quite well known as a gay-rights activist and it wasn't a secret that he was homosexual.

Roberto and Eric first met in an amusing way. They were both living in the east end of Mexico City at the time. One day, Eric's cat appeared at Roberto's door. Of all the doorsteps the cat could have selected, she chose Roberto's. Roberto already had cats and didn't want to acquire another one. Their common love of felines became the motivation for them getting to know each other. I understood from our conversation that they had been a couple for a long time. Same-sex marriage is legal in Mexico, and they had been planning their wedding before fleeing to Canada.

Up until this point in our conversation, the three of us were sitting, chatting, and enjoying our lunch and the sunshine. I learned that Eric, in his early thirties, was a few years older than Roberto. In Mexico, Roberto was working as a server in a restaurant, while Eric was doing security sales. Eric holds an engineering degree as well as a master's degree in business administration in marketing.

The mood changed dramatically when I asked them what precipitated their move to seek asylum in Canada. They became quiet and glanced back and forth at each other. Roberto had a look of horror in his eyes. I could see that he was holding back tears. I am sure the silence only lasted for a few seconds, but it felt like forever. Then Eric began to speak. His eyes were so intense that I couldn't move.

The last six months before they fled to Canada were extremely difficult. Eric, Roberto, and their collection of cats were the only ones residing in their home. Someone had been secretly sneaking fibreglass into the ventilation system of their house. The dust is very fine with chards of glass, and they didn't notice it at first, although they were both experiencing itchy skin and rashes, and it was also affecting the cats. By the time they recognized that something was seriously wrong, the fine powder had infiltrated the entire house. When they sought professional help, they learned that their air filters were full of fibreglass, and they had to have a completely new filter system installed. The damage was extensive, and they depleted their savings in making their home safe again. Friends provided them with some financial support to assist with payment of the bills, but it wasn't enough.

Around the same time, someone was placing black widow spiders into the house to harm them, but mostly to kill their cats. They believed that Eric's family, particularly his grandmother, was responsible for both attacks. There was also a narrative being spread in the community that Eric and Roberto were drug dealers, making them an even larger target for violence. Eric strongly suspected that his grandmother initiated those rumours. She had made it clear on multiple occasions that the family would be better off if Eric were dead and had implied that she might even do it herself.

Roberto eventually lost his job because of the fibreglass dust which had permeated their clothing and bedding, even their hair. It was difficult if not impossible to wash all of it away. Since he was a restaurant server, the concern expressed by the manager was that the material might get into the food and cause harm to customers. Roberto was told he could return to his job when there was no more fibreglass on him or any of his clothing.

Eric and Roberto eventually fled from the house, and they were forced to move five different times during a short period of time. They were constantly on the move because they were repeatedly being stalked and threatened. They were being relentlessly chased by motorcycles, and the drivers always seemed to know their whereabouts. In desperation, they began living in their van which was obviously mobile and could change locations frequently. They later learned that there was a tracker device on the van and possibly on their phone. They were literally being hunted down, and had no option but to keep running, without a bed, and with little sleep. They lived in constant fear for their lives.

Finally, on the brink of exhaustion and unable to function, they stayed at an Airbnb where they could sleep on a bed. The horrific course of events that followed became the catalyst for why they fled their home country. Neither Eric nor Roberto's memories of the events are clear, as they had both been drugged. Eric woke to find he was nude and tied to a chair with plastic cuffs. He had severe pain near his liver, suggesting he may have been beaten. Roberto was being pinned down and repeatedly raped with objects and hands. The perpetrators, essentially terrorists, were forcing pills down Roberto's throat to keep him drugged. He was not entirely conscious. Eric dislocated his shoulder struggling frantically to break free from the chair and help Roberto. Shockingly, one of Eric's aunts was in the room taking pictures and videos of Roberto being raped. Eric remembers that she was smiling and seemed to be enjoying these gruesome acts of violence. When and why these horrible people left is also unclear. Likely both men were unconscious because of the drugs they were forced to ingest.

As soon as he had the strength to free himself, Eric brought Roberto to the hospital, who was unable to stand, and whose body was shaking uncontrollably. His eyes were continuously moving around in different directions up and down, as well as side to side. Eric made a statement to hospital staff that Roberto had been sexually abused, that they had both been assaulted and drugged, and that Roberto was repeatedly forced to ingest pills. Hospital staff were asking Eric how to contact Roberto's family. They did not acknowledge Eric's relationship with Roberto, even though he informed them that they were life partners and engaged to marry. A large man, either a doctor or someone impersonating one, punched Eric in his side and two other people, who Eric assumed were hospital staff because of their uniforms, were laughing about the nature of Eric and Roberto's relationship. Eric felt that the nurses were behaving in a very strange manner.

Eric was informed that Roberto was not expected to live but he was not permitted into the room with him because he was not immediate family. He could hear people's voices from where he was sitting in the waiting room. It sounded to him like they were planning how they might be able to ensure Roberto died, to effectively murder him. They also discussed how it would not be long before Roberto would be dead and Eric would be jailed so the family would be finally rid of them both. Eric became suspicious that his family had alerted the hospital that they would be arriving, and that they had paid the staff or people to pose as hospital staff to cause Roberto even more harm. His family was aware that the best way to harm him and cause him pain would be to murder his beloved life partner.

Eric was convinced that Roberto was not safe in the hospital and asked for him to be immediately discharged. He was informed that since he had made serious allegations of assault, including sexual assault, that he would first need to speak with police about these crimes because the hospital had sent official documentation about Roberto's injuries to the police.

Eric went to the police, who were obviously expecting him. But when he explained what had happened, they tried to arrest him for the rape and abuse of Roberto. Clearly the hospital staff had purposefully filed inaccurate information so that Eric would be thrown into jail. Eric recognized that the entire situation was orchestrated, so he recorded all his interactions with them and began to live stream what was happening with his phone. This meant that the police couldn't really jail him or cause him bodily harm without it being documented, and any arrest would be unlawful. Eric fled and returned to the hospital.

Quite suspiciously, many of the hospital staff that were previously with Roberto had now disappeared. Eric doesn't know if they were corrupt staff who fled, or if they were paid people posing as hospital staff. But he knew his grandmother and other family members were at the source of the treatment they received while at the hospital.

When Eric was exiting the hospital, Roberto was still not lucid and could not walk. Surprisingly, Eric went to his mother's house, who permitted them both to stay for two days. Eric says his mother did provide care for Roberto while they were there. Roberto continued to bleed for several days every time he went to the bathroom. Although his mother did not approve of homosexuals, she was apparently not an active participant of the family conspiracy to eradicate both men.

Eric was well-known in the community for his "gay" activism, so he handed their story with recorded documentation to a news reporter, who published it. While they didn't believe it would make a difference to the overall situation in the long run, because police were corrupt and would not have investigated the alleged crimes, Eric felt it might buy them some time. He hoped the abuse and stalking might temporarily cease. He believed the printed story would also come in handy when they were seeking asylum.

At one point when I was listening to Eric speak, I blurted out a swear word because I was so shocked at their story. I immediately apologized to them for doing so. Eric broke the tension by explaining that when they speak Spanish, the syntax is as follows: Noun-Verb-Curse or Curse-Noun-Verb, or any combination, but at least one curse word is required. Eric's use of humour, perhaps as a coping mechanism, was much needed and appreciated, as the retelling of these events was obviously traumatic for both men, but especially for Roberto.

After leaving Eric's mother's house, they spent a few weeks in an LGBTQ+ refugee shelter in Mexico, although they were not refugees. There they spoke with someone who knew about refugee programs. Eric explained to them that his family was trying to kill them both because of their sexual orientation, and they wanted to exit Mexico and seek asylum elsewhere. Apparently, these professionals suggested the two men try to come to Canada. Eric and Roberto did some research on the internet and believed this might be a viable option for them. They sold the appliances from the house they had initially fled from, which gave them some funds. All their running and repeated moving as fugitives had depleted their savings.

Roberto had to obtain a passport before they could leave, but Eric already had one. Eric also had an American Visa, which he had to surrender when he entered Canada. As soon as they could, they purchased one-way tickets to Canada.

When they landed in Toronto they were "super scared." They identified themselves immediately to someone at border control and asked for asylum. He escorted them into a separate room where an immigration officer of the Canada Border Services Agency greeted them. This officer was apparently gentle and caring. He offered to get them an interpreter at no charge to them, which they declined. He also commented that they must be tired and offered them tea and water. Eric and Roberto were completely exhausted both from the entire ordeal, but also because they had not slept for the three days prior to their departure. Eric said they were completely shocked that they were being treated with such dignity and respect. They found that everyone they interacted with, including police, were so nice, in contrast to the treatment they were given by the authorities back home.

While at the airport, they were fingerprinted and had their pictures taken. The interview, which included a security screening, involved them completing an application package, which took several hours. When everything they were required to do was finished, they became Refugee Claimants, which is a legal status in Canada. They were shocked that it happened on the spot! Those who are Refugee Claimants remain in Canada while waiting for their claim to be heard by the Refugee Protection Division of the Immigration and Refugee Board of Canada. They were informed this might take up to twenty-four months to be scheduled, but that they could apply for a work permit during that time, which would probably be processed in about six to nine months.

From the airport, Eric and Roberto were first assigned to a shelter near Billy Bishop Airport where they were provided with food and a bed. They were finally able to get some sleep. They remained there for seven weeks before they were reassigned to a second shelter in Scarborough, which was for refugees only. They had brought clothes with them, but most of them had to be destroyed, because they still were full of the fibreglass dust.

Eric and Roberto began volunteering at a non-profit organization for Latinos living with HIV/AIDS while they were awaiting their work permits. These are incredible young men who, if given the opportunity, free of persecution, will make a difference in the world.

So far, Eric and Roberto seem to be managing life in Toronto. They were able to find a new place of their own to live around the same time as their work permits were issued. They have an apartment inside of a townhouse in East York. They feel very safe there and have hung a huge Pride flag on their porch. They are not concerned that it isn't Pride month. They want everyone to know they are here, and they are queer!

Obviously, there are cultural differences for them to navigate. A funny story—the first time they took public transportation in Toronto they purchased a transit card and took the bus. However, they were almost unable to exit the bus because they didn't know they had to push the button, or the bars on the door for them to open.

At this point in time, they believe they will remain in Canada for their mental and physical health in addition to their safety. Eric is not in touch with anyone in his family and what they endured still haunts them. When they first arrived, Roberto suffered very high anxiety and almost any noise made him nervous. He would also wake up petrified and screaming during the night and suffered from bad dreams. Eric says Roberto doesn't scream nearly as often now and seems to be much less anxious, but he continues to deal with post-traumatic stress.

I was moved to tears many times while listening to them speak. It was extremely difficult not to cry. I had and still have no way to process what they were telling me. I quietly reached out and held Roberto's hands while Eric was describing the rape and abuse. The pain in his eyes was piercing. The intensity of what was happening among us was so great that our server came to our table to ask if we were okay, and he didn't mean with our food. I motioned to him not to interrupt. When Eric appeared to have exhausted speaking, and there was silence, I didn't know what to do. I told them I was so very sorry that this had happened and that they were both incredibly brave to have come forward with their painful story.

We had long finished eating. So, I offered them the possibility of ordering dessert. They were both incredibly delighted by the choices on the dessert menu, and so thrilled by the treat, that I was reminded that these were two young men who were simply trying to live, just like anyone else.

Roberto and Eric are the only two people I interviewed who permitted use of their real names. There was both strength and defiance in their eyes when they told me they did not want to use pseudonyms. I got the impression that this was one way they had of asserting that nobody was going to oppress or harm them ever again. When Eric told me his name, I was surprised by it because the name "Eric" does not sound to me like a Spanish name. He clarified that his parents named him after the Prince in *The Little Mermaid* cartoon. This amused me greatly, because I had named Ariella, whose journey also appears in the book, after the same movie. I shared this story with them, and they were amused too. In a strange way, this enabled them to feel connected to someone else who arrived in Toronto as a refugee because of their sexual orientation or gender identity.

Although it hasn't been long since I interviewed these men, I can provide an update. I was extremely moved when they attended the launch of my book *Surviving the Closet*[28] in the Fall of 2023, three months after we first met. I was delighted to see them. Ironically, they said they wanted to support my endeavours and they were excitedly anticipating when *their* book would be published! I noted that they both looked well-rested, healthy, and very happy.

#

From a purely superficial perspective, things don't appear to be that difficult in Mexico for people who are 2SLGBTQ+. As of 2022, same-sex marriage is legal in all thirty-two states and according to the Human Rights Watch World Reports,[29,30] just over half of the states have laws that permit people who are transgender to have their names and gender changed on their birth certificate. Surgery is not required. As of May 2023, a non-binary gender is legally recognized. Pride parades and celebrations occur in the larger cities. Discrimination against people because of sexual orientation and gender identity is illegal. Openly gay people can serve in the military, although people who are transgender are still banned.

At the same time, Mexico is known to commit numerous human rights violations such as torture and enforced disappearances.[29,30] Disappearances, which may not have anything to do with people who are 2SLGBTQ+, are not just orchestrated by criminal groups or organized crime but by police as well as the military, and there seems to be impunity. Mexico is known to be one of the most dangerous and deadly countries worldwide for journalists and people defending human rights and attacks on these people are widespread and common.[29,30] Gender-based and sexual violence occurs at disturbing levels.[29,30] Violent crimes are at an all-time high in the country. It is estimated that over ninety percent of crimes are never reported, and even when they are, many are never investigated and most go unresolved. The criminal justice system in Mexico does not protect victims of violent crimes or human rights violations. Corruption is present everywhere on multiple levels.

Ultimately, even when the laws were technically on Roberto and Eric's side, they had no recourse or protection when they were aggressively persecuted by family members and their lives were in danger. Police and even some medical staff condoned and participated in the persecution. They knew when they fled to Canada that they would be completely at the mercy of the immigration officers they met when they landed. But it didn't matter. They understood that for them, remaining in Mexico would mean certain death.

There is no gray area here. Roberto and Eric were denied their human rights, and they were tortured and hunted down like animals because of their sexual orientation. They were dying to be gay.

Maryam:
Nowhere to Run

Maryam is a cisgender, lesbian woman of twenty-one years of age at the time of her interview. However, she did not share with me her journey to Canada as a refugee to find freedom living as an "out" lesbian. She does not tell a story of escaping from an oppressive country to find a better, more authentic life. Maryam has lived in Canada for as long as she can remember. She immigrated to Canada with her parents from South Asia when she was barely three years old, and she was raised in the Greater Toronto Area (GTA). Her younger siblings were all born in Canada.

Why would I include Maryam's story in a book about 2SLGBTQ+ people who have found freedom in Canada after first entering this country as refugees? There is no dancing around the answer to make it less harsh: as mentioned earlier in the book, living in Canada or any country offering protection does not necessarily guarantee that people with non-conventional sexual orientations, gender expressions, or gender identities will be free. Or even safe.

Despite growing up Canadian, Maryam lives in constant fear that her parents and religious community will learn her truth: why she immerses herself in her studies and has no time to think about finding a husband, and why she will remain in school for as long as her father will permit. Maryam fears that if her parents knew she was gay, she would be banished from her family. She also fears for her life and believes that there is a very real possibility that her parents or a relative would kill her or arrange to have her murdered if they learned she was a lesbian. To her family, there is no honour in being gay, only humiliation. And even though they are quiet about it, they believe in honour killings.

Maryam's parents identify with a culture and religion where any sexual activity outside of traditional, heterosexual marriage is considered illegal and immoral. Her parents believe sex between two men to be abhorrent. They view gay men as lower than animals for ignoring God's teachings and that the punishment for being a male homosexual should be death.

Maryam had never heard her parents mention sex between two women while growing up. In fact, she was not even aware that it was possible for two women to engage in sex until she was in university. When she first learned of actual sex acts between women, she asked her parents about it. They responded that sex between two women was not actually possible, because there is no penis involved, and sex necessitates penal penetration. They also explained their belief that two women touching each other was something that originated in Western societies, and is not found in their home country, or in any country that is primarily Muslim. Women who engage in such acts are essentially guilty of the sin of masturbation, which they consider to be haram (forbidden according to the laws of Islam).

In elementary and secondary school, Maryam's parents never permitted her or her siblings to attend any classes that discussed sex, sexuality, or even puberty. From a very young age, she was instructed to leave the classroom whenever a teacher talked about people's bodies or any physical contact between people. She was essentially raised in a bubble of her parent's beliefs and values, which were also shared by the families with which her family socialized.

In Maryam's traditions, men are the heads of the household and the guardians of women. Women have an essential and honourable role to play; they raise the children and take care of the home. Her father believes that education is good for women, because this means they can raise smarter children, especially boys. But they should not use their education to find work outside of the home. He considered this an unworthy and unnecessary distraction.

With respect to women having jobs, her father has recently altered his view somewhat. He now believes that it might be acceptable for a woman to leave her home to work for pay, if her husband is unable to support his family in this difficult economy. However, he would never have wanted this for his own wife. And he does not want that for his daughters.

Virtually all of Maryam's family friends embrace the same fundamental belief as her parents. Although they reside in different neighbourhoods in the GTA, most of them originate from the same part of the world, and they attend the same place of worship.

Maryam is highly animated, with a witty sense of humour. She speaks very quickly and with great expression. She is enviably articulate, and unlike most of the people her age, the word "like" is not sprinkled throughout every sentence. She never uses word fillers such as "um" and "ah," and she doesn't use profanity. Maryam does not tell me her story in a linear fashion. Rather, she creates vivid little vignettes with her words.

When I met Maryam for her interview, I asked her to tell me a bit about herself. She remembers attending a neighbourhood BBQ in the summer before she entered senior kindergarten, so she believes she must have been around five at the time. She thinks that her family was the only Muslim family in attendance, because she remembers that her mother was the only woman wearing a hijab, and she was the only little girl whose head was similarly covered. Maryam had been warned by her mother before they arrived at the BBQ not to get her special dress dirty, and she promised her that she wouldn't.

It was a scorching hot day, and the children were all chasing each other around the yard playing tag. Maryam promptly stripped down to her undershirt and underpants so that she could run unrestricted and wouldn't get her fancy party dress dirty. "There I was, running around the yard in my underwear, but with my head still covered."

At the time, Maryam says literally all the adults at the party laughed, except for her father. It must have been an incredibly cute, amusing sight. However, when they returned home, her father scolded her harshly, and warned her about the importance of modesty. He also reprimanded her mother for laughing. Maryam had no idea why he was so angry. She was told not to get her dress dirty, and she didn't. She had done exactly what she was told.

She does recall always hating wearing dresses. They made her feel uncomfortable. To this day, if she must dress in a more formal manner, she prefers wearing a traditional outfit from her birth country to Western clothing, because at least those outfits are not so constricting. She explains that "it feels just like wearing a baggy tunic with pajama pants, only classier."

Maryam's family does not require her to wear dresses. However, she must dress modestly, covering her shoulders, arms, and legs, even when the weather is hot. And they demand she cover her head unless she is at home with her immediate family. Maryam clarifies that contrary to popular belief, wearing the hijab is a cultural, not a religious, requirement. She personally likes to cover her head. She feels it empowers her to take control of her own body and send the message that she is not available for the sexual pleasure of men.

Maryam described herself as a very physically active child. When she was five or six, her parents registered her in soccer to wear off some of her excess energy. She absolutely loved it and enthusiastically played the game until the age of twelve. She was also extremely skilled at it, being a striker and scoring many goals. She especially loved competing in tournaments, which she was permitted to do if they did not fall on a Friday, and she was still able to pray five times each day. It was great, until she experienced her first menstrual period. After that, her parents forced her to quit the sport. They felt that a girl of her age should not be engaging in this type of activity because it was not becoming of a woman. Her father said that her shirt clung too close to her body when she was running, which was immodest, and therefore immoral. Maryam was devastated.

Maryam remembers wanting to kiss girls as early as Grade Two. But she somehow recognized that her longing to kiss a girl was different from the kisses her girlfriends bestowed upon each other every morning when they first arrived at school. Maryam kept these feelings a secret. She mentioned them to no one.

Often, when she and her friends played dress up, Maryam would volunteer to play the husband. This somehow made it more acceptable for her to hold and cuddle the other girls. She told me that she used to refer to baseball caps as "husband hats." Her parents discouraged her from taking on the role of the husband, but for some reason unknown to Maryam, they did not forbid it.

As Maryam got older, she adored middle school because the girls only wanted to be with other girls. They giggled together, hugged, and held hands. They hated all the smelly boys and thought that girls should rule the classroom. Maryam couldn't have agreed more. It also pleased her parents that she did not wish to play or interact with any of the boys. Maryam longed to experience a sleepover with her girlfriends, but her parents never permitted this.

As preteens, the other girls at school began to swoon over pop singers and movie stars. Not Maryam. Her first crush was her Grade Six teacher, a favourite teacher at the school. Maryam remembers admiring the teacher's neck. This teacher usually wore skirts that fell to just below the knee, and collared shirts. She had a casual style and apparently always kept the top two buttons of her shirts undone. This, according to Maryam, made the perfect frame for her elegant, willowy neck and shapely collar bones.

Maryam also remembers noticing the frilly lace of her teacher's brassieres when she bent over to pick up papers, or to check someone's homework. Some of her teacher's bras were pink, blue, or even patterned. It was positively scandalous! Maryam remembers asking questions she already knew the answers to just so her teacher would lean over her desk and take a look at her work. "Her bras had no resemblance to my mother's industrial strength white and beige ones. They took my breath away."

Maryam offered to help the teacher at recess and after school, and the other children accused her of being the teacher's pet. Maryam didn't mind in the least. She did anything she could to be physically near to this woman. Maryam didn't know what this attraction meant, but she knew to keep those feelings to herself.

Maryam was eleven when she first learned about honour killings.

The sixteen-year-old daughter of a family that attended the same Mosque as Maryam's family was complaining about having to dress modestly. As well, she repeatedly spoke to boys outside of the classroom after her father had explicitly forbidden her to do so. She was also refusing to cover her head.

Maryam overheard her parents talking one evening about how this girl's father had lost control of his daughter, and he needed to teach her a lesson. Her mother said that the girl was tarnishing the family's name and causing them great embarrassment.

One Saturday evening, this girl apparently told her parents she was going to see a movie with some female friends, when she was really going to a school dance. The school dance was, of course, completely out of the question. Absolutely forbidden. The girl's father dropped her off and picked her up at the movie theatre at the prearranged times, completely oblivious to his daughter's lie. She might have gotten away with it, if not for Facebook.

The girl's older brother, who was also in high school, happened to see her picture posted on Facebook. Someone from the school had posted some arbitrary pictures of the dance. His sister was only in the background, and only part of her face was visible, but she was clearly identifiable.

The girl was pictured smiling in a group of both boys and girls. They all had their arms wrapped around each other, not in any sexual way, but much like a sports team when they pose for a team picture. Still, being in mixed company and allowing herself to be touched by males who were not family members was sinful, according to this family. The girl had lied about her whereabouts, and perhaps worse, her head was completely uncovered. Her brother felt he had no choice but to make his parents aware of these reprehensible and sinful behaviours. That girl's punishment landed her in the hospital.

Maryam attended the same elementary school as this girl's younger sister. The main story that was circulating around the schoolyard was that the older sister was in the hospital after tripping and falling down an entire flight of stairs at home. She was suffering from some serious injuries. However, a few of the children at school were whispering that the fall was not an accident, and that the older brother had thrown his sister down the stairs in anger.

Maryam's mother had a completely different version of the story altogether. She told Maryam that the girl's parents did the right thing, and that she had to be disciplined. According to Maryam's mother, the girl got what she deserved. Her mother's exact words, "If not for Allah, she would be dead."

The conflicting stories confused Maryam, so she begged the girl's sister at school to tell her what had really happened. The girl made her promise that she would never tell. Her sister had not fallen down the stairs at all. She had been beaten by her father as a punishment for disrespectful and immoral behaviour. The little sister was instructed by her parents to tell anyone that inquired about her big sister's injuries that she had observed the tragic accident of her sister slipping and rolling all the way down the entire flight of stairs.

She regurgitated to Maryam her parent's comments that Canadians are too lenient and permissive with their children, especially their daughters. Canadians do not appreciate the gravity of girls remaining chaste, or the pressure that is on their families to uphold their status within their community. Her friend also explained quite matter-of-factly that her father had no choice but to protect the family's honour. Her sister needed to be punished. The sanctity of the family depended upon it.

The little girl confided in Maryam that she feared that if there was a "next time," her sister would be killed, if not by her father, by her brother. She called this an honour killing.

Maryam always understood that killing people was wrong. She knew it was against the law. When she questioned her mother about this, her mother answered that honour killings were different, and that their people had their own laws. She emphasized that it was not wrong to kill someone if the intention was to fulfill the obligations of the religion and to protect the family. Maryam was horrified. She was also very relieved that she had no interest in attending school dances.

Maryam was a high school student the second time she heard about honour killings. This time, a young Muslim woman was murdered by her brother after he found her in a parked car kissing a boy, presumably her unsanctioned boyfriend. The brother was charged and convicted of her murder. But he never showed any remorse. He refused to apologize for protecting the good name of his family. He was proud of his actions.

Maryam's voice was barely audible when she told me that her parents agreed with the brother. In their eyes, that girl deserved to die.

There are no words to describe the pain on Maryam's face when she told me this story. It was clear she was thinking that the same thing could happen to her. She didn't need to express it out loud. But for Maryam, the person she would be kissing, would be another woman.

The Government of Canada Department of Justice website has documented known honour killings in Canada since 2002. Most of the deceased seem to be young women desiring to wear Westernized clothing and no head covering. I can only guess how many injuries or beatings never get reported or are not recognized as having the preservation of the family's honour as the motive for the crime.

As stated, Maryam has never minded wearing the hijab. She always wore it, even while playing soccer, and she continues to wear it to this day. It gives her parents great bragging rights within their social circle that Maryam kept her head covered throughout her teenage years without even one complaint. Her parents believe she is an incredible role model for her younger siblings. It hurts Maryam deeply to think that she might one day be considered a source of humiliation for them.

Maryam was an outstanding student throughout high school. When she was in Grade Ten, she wanted to partner with a boy named Rob for the junior science fair. Rob was white, Canadian-born, and Christian. And he was a science star. Her parents reluctantly agreed.

Maryam and Rob diligently worked on their experiments before and after school, and during lunch. When they needed extra time, Maryam was forbidden to go to Rob's house, so Rob came to Maryam's. They worked at the kitchen table and there was always a parent chaperone present.

Maryam followed her parent's restrictions for working with Rob without complaint. She was excited about the project and the prospect of coming first in their school. She knew the work was of very high-level calibre, and they were easily selected to represent their high school at a regional science fair. The science teacher told them that they had a great chance of receiving a gold medal.

On the day of the science fair, other students from her school came to view all the projects and to cheer for Maryam and Rob. Maryam's parents and siblings were all in attendance. It was going to be a great day.

Maryam will never forget that first science fair. She won a gold medal, and their science project received the highest award of the day. After the winners were announced, Rob excitedly hugged her, as did some of the other students. Everyone was elated. They also hugged Rob. It was a great honour for the school. Maryam was thrilled and assumed her parents would be proud of her.

When Maryam and her family returned home, her father requested that her mother take the younger children upstairs. He then proceeded to slap Maryam across the face with the back of his hand so hard that she fell to the floor. He told her that she should not have let Rob, and those other boys, hold their bodies so close to hers.

"I was stunned. I had done absolutely everything my parents had asked."

Instead of apologizing and begging for forgiveness, she challenged her father. She explained that those were simply congratulatory hugs, and completely innocent. She told him that he was overreacting, and that he had misunderstood the gesture. Her father's response was to remove his belt and whip her for disrespecting him. He struck her repeatedly until her garments were ripped and hanging like rags, and he was sweating and exhausted. During the entire ordeal, Maryam's mother did nothing to stop it. Maryam tells me that the scars that remain on her back from the beating are deep and numerous. But the scars of her mother not defending her run much deeper. And they will never fade.

That was the only time Maryam was ever hit by her father. She made a promise to herself that she would never again put herself in a situation that would anger him. However, now she wonders if she can keep this promise. She can only speculate about her father's reaction should he discover her sexual orientation. And she fears for her safety.

Maryam never really struggled with her sexuality in high school. She always knew she was gay, even before she understood the word for it. What she struggled with was the reality that she may never experience a gay relationship. She always assumed that she would eventually marry a man and have children.

Maryam and her siblings are not permitted to use the Internet in their bedrooms at home. They are required to do homework in the kitchen or other common areas of the house. Maryam thinks this is ludicrous, especially at her age. She is an adult. But she keeps her opinion to herself. She is always very careful not to open any websites on her laptop that might be considered inappropriate or immoral by her family. She has never looked at Western bathing suits on either males or females, and she would never purchase underwear online.

Despite her understanding that she was sexually and romantically attracted to other girls as a teenager, Maryam remained confused about the logistics of lesbian sex. As far as she knew, sex needed to involve a penis, and a woman didn't have one. She didn't know about oral sex, and she was unaware of alternative ways of achieving sexual gratification. As difficult as it is to believe, she had never heard the word orgasm.

Maryam acquired some cryptic information about homosexuality on the Internet when she was at the public library, but it was really very limited. Mostly, she learned about two men having anal intercourse. It was sex because it involved a penis penetrating something.

When she imagined herself with another girl, she thought about kissing them on the lips, and fondling their breasts. This was sexual enough. Beyond that, she was unaware of any other forms of sexual gratification between two women. She said that at the time, she didn't even possess the correct vocabulary to enable her to research and understand lesbian sex.

When Maryam was in Grade Eleven and Twelve, she devoted all her time to her schoolwork. Dating was a non-issue, because her parents would not have allowed her to date, and she wasn't romantically interested in boys anyway. She knew that dating another girl would not be an option. Besides, she didn't know any other lesbians. Most of her friends were from strict religious families. She wasn't comfortable discussing sexuality of any kind with them or anyone else.

Maryam graduated high school with exceptional grades and received a generous entrance scholarship to a university near her home. There were no other options for her, since her parents believe that it is unacceptable for girls to live away from their parent's home unless they are married.

University has been educational for Maryam in many ways, and not just from an academic perspective. During her very first year at university, she discovered the 2SLGBTQ+ student group/club, which was in the same building as one of her classes. It took her two months before she had the courage to walk into that office. But she is grateful that she did. She was surprised to discover other gay students who are Muslim and astonished to learn that not all of them are in the closet. Here, she was able to fill in the blanks with factual knowledge.

For the first time in her life, Maryam was able to have open conversations about sex, sexuality, and her body. It was life-altering. Some of the other gay, Muslim students share similar stories to hers. Others have families that accept them. Many of the students she has met through the 2SLGBTQ+ group have become her closest friends and greatest allies. But she says that some of them will never meet her family. She will only introduce female friends who wear a hijab.

Through this group at university, Maryam learned of a Queer Muslim organization, *Salaam Canada*, and other supports and safe spaces for Muslims who identify as being 2SLGBTQ+. Maryam says she benefited greatly from their web-based educational resources. Sadly, *Salaam Canada* officially closed in August 2022. However, she is now familiar with websites from outside of Canada that reveal that some Muslims are supportive of progressive ideas and do not seek to harm but include those who identify as having a non-conventional sexual orientation or gender identity or expression. It gives her great comfort to know that it is possible for her to be homosexual, and still maintain her faith. Maryam makes it very clear that Islam is not about hate. She has difficulty reconciling her understanding of Islam with some of her parent's deep-rooted beliefs. She struggles with the question of whether Allah can love people who are gay. She hopes that he can.

Maryam recently earned her university degree and will soon begin graduate school. Her grades are quite high, and her aspiration is to study medicine. But her parents are against this. They have expressed their concern that if she becomes a doctor, she will have difficulty finding a husband because she will be so old when she finishes school. "It would be a welcome relief to be considered too old to marry. Perhaps then, I can get my own place and live how I please."

Her parents have told her that they will not force her into an arranged marriage. They will gift her the privilege of marrying for love. Of course, their underlying assumption is that she will marry within her culture and religion. And they definitely assume that she will marry a man.

Maryam's parents expect her to continue to live at home while in graduate school. There are other girls at her Mosque whose families have permitted them to attend graduate or professional school outside of Toronto, but Maryam doesn't know if her parents would ever bend on this rule. They have recently permitted her to take an outside job at a coffee shop to help cover some of her university costs. This has given her some flexibility in meeting up with people.

Maryam has yet to have her first real sexual experience with a woman. But she explained that it is not unusual for someone her age in her culture to have no sexual experience, even with an opposite sex partner.

There was a glint in her eyes when she said that her goal in the first year of graduate studies is to find herself a girlfriend who also wears hijab. "Insha'Allah," she says with a smile. *If God is willing.*

Maryam's cheery disposition belies her situation. By her own admission, she is completely trapped. She loves her family and believes that her parents are good people. At the same time, she longs to explore a whole different world, where she will be free to love. She is committed to remaining a Muslim and emphasizes that many of the rules her family strictly adheres to are based more in culture than in religion.

She takes comfort in the knowledge that people born in countries of the world that hate and persecute 2SLGBTQ+ people are permitted to enter Canada and can hopefully live an authentic life. She absolutely supports the importance of telling their stories. However, she believes very strongly that it would be a great disservice to the many people in Canada who live her reality by suggesting that all 2SLGBTQ+ people are free and safe here.

At Maryam's request, I have not named her country of birth. But really, the actual name of the country is not that important. Her story could have been written about someone living in Canada who came from any number of countries where the primary religion denounces, demonizes, and strives to eradicate homosexuality. While the religion of Maryam's family is Islam, the country doesn't have to be a Muslim state. Families from cultures around the world where women are oppressed and treated as property make things particularly difficult for lesbian women.

Unlike Maryam, some women in Canada still do not have access to education beyond what is mandated by law, and their father or husband become their only source of income. A woman who is assigned a husband in an arranged marriage at a very young age will not likely have the means to survive without that husband, whether or not she was forced into the marriage, or willingly agreed to it.

Tragically, some 2SLGBTQ+ women must fear for their safety despite residing in a country that strives to protect people of different sexual orientations, gender identities, or expressions. This problem is largely hidden from the broader community, and it is easy to hold on to the false belief that everyone is safe and included.

Even in less restrictive environments, religion and culture often pressure women to marry and have children, regardless of what these women might choose if they were given the opportunity to genuinely decide for themselves. Many women are raised from a very young age to believe that their only role is to take care of a husband, home, and family. Their family's acceptance within their community, as well as their own self-worth, is dependent on upholding this way of life.

The strong pull of religion at the centre of family is not unique to Islam. There are multiple religions that are completely intertwined with family, and some women are not willing or able to assume the risk of being alienated or ex-communicated from their families and the religious or ethnic communities that define them.

> I would like you to relay the message that people who believe coming out is not really an issue anymore are wrong. Coming out as gay is not feasible for many women today, even in Canada. Women just like me.

Maryam has now come to the realization that for her, living an authentic life would most likely mean that she would no longer be able to see her parents and siblings again. She would have to disappear. Just as if she had fled her country as a refugee.

In time, it is possible that immigrants like Maryam's parents will begin to see that they can still worship the way they choose and dress the way they'd like, while embracing the respect for diversity and the provision of human rights that Canada affords. Or is supposed to afford. But for now, they are stuck fast to their beliefs.

Maryam chose her own pseudonym for this book. She explained that she selected this name because Mary/Mariam/Maryam, as the mother of Jesus, is one of the most revered people in her religion. She is also apparently the only woman whose actual name is explicitly mentioned in the Quran. According to Maryam, women are talked about, but not named. They are referenced in terms of their relationship as someone's mother or wife. Maryam does not wish to be defined or remembered this way. She refuses to be nameless.

I have been in touch with Maryam since her initial interview. However, for confidentiality reasons and her safety, she has requested that I not provide any information about where she is living and what she is doing.

Perhaps one day, Maryam will be as free as the little girl who once ran around outside on a hot summer day, hijab flying in the wind, wearing only her underwear. But for now, she has nowhere to run.

#

Countries that have Sharia law as their entire or partial legal system can be particularly harsh in their treatment of people who are gay.[31] This includes countries such as Afghanistan, Bangladesh, Iran, Iraq, Mauritania, Palestine, Saudi Arabia, Sudan, and Syria, and this is not an exhaustive list. In these countries, when someone is beaten or purposefully injured by family members because of their sexuality, the victim may have no legal recourse. Police do not typically intervene in issues that are related to personal family matters, especially when related to sexual orientation. Even in countries that do not have Sharia law, culturally, people may adhere to these religious laws. Under this system, homosexual acts are criminalized with punishments that can include ending the person's life.

Many countries are both homophobic and transphobic, but threats of persecution because of gender identity do not necessarily follow a country's viewpoint on homosexuality. Countries such as Saudi Arabia and Egypt, which are both exceedingly homophobic, are not always cruel or unkind towards people who are transgender. A rationale that has been postulated by others is that if a person is having "sex-reassignment" or gender-confirming surgery, they will now become heterosexual. However, this is a false assumption, and someone who is transgender can have any sexual orientation identity.

Bangladesh, a country that forbids same-sex activity and aggressively discriminates against people who are homosexual, has legally recognized a third-gender category for people they refer to as *hijras*, people who are neither male nor female. Bolivia, which does not recognize same-sex marriage and has a similar viewpoint to Bangladesh about homosexuality, permits people to change their gender on their legal documents. Even in Turkmenistan, where homophobic violence and discrimination is quite common, transgender people are afforded the legal right to change their gender without having any surgery.

Surprisingly, Iran, which is known for inhumane treatment of homosexuals unless they are from very wealthy families, is fairly accepting of people who are transgender, provided they undergo surgery on their genitals. This has been the status quo there for over thirty-five years, and Iran has the second most sex-reassignment surgeries in the world.[32] Thailand reportedly has the highest. Unfortunately, a greater number of "bottom" surgeries is not necessarily a positive thing. It has been reported in multiple sources that gay men in Iran sometimes feel pressure to undergo gender-confirming surgery even when they are not transgender, so they can be safe. From a social perspective, it is better for them to be transexual than to be gay, since penalties for people who are homosexual in Iran are harsh and can include death.

Unfortunately, even though Maryam lives in a country considered neither homophobic nor transphobic, she still cannot escape such engrained hate from her family's loyalty to the beliefs of their country of birth.

You Can Call Me Mo

While I watch Mo's face and hear his voice, I'm listening to a translator. The language they are speaking is not Mo's mother tongue, it is Russian, a language he seems to know quite fluently because of his country's proximity to Russia. I can't help wondering how much information is lost as Mo's thoughts go into a second language, and then get filtered through the translator. At Mo's request, we did not use a professional translator. He was petrified that the professional translator might know his family, might disclose where he is living, and convey the information that he is gay. I assure him that professional translators are bound by a strict code of ethics, and they will not share what he shares with anyone. But he is too afraid. So, at his request, we use a friend of his who speaks many languages, one of which is Russian. However, his friend has only been speaking English for two years. I am grateful he has agreed to facilitate our conversation, but how do I know that these are really Mo's words?

I can't know.

The anguish on Mo's face is clear as he speaks. Sometimes he cries. When he cries, the translator cries too, and I am not sure what to do. There are no rules for writing this book. Even though I have interviewed others before him, I have no guidelines to follow. Mo's emotions are still raw, and he is suffering from post-traumatic stress. He has been in Toronto for only six months, and he is so very young, technically still a teenager.

I assure him that he can stop the interview, we can meet another time, or not at all. But these are not options. Words I do not understand are pouring out of him like water gushing from a broken fire hydrant. I am afraid to breathe for fear I might drown in his pain. I feel selfish and privileged. The pain is his. This is not about me. Anything I could possibly feel is miniscule in comparison.

At times, we are all crying. The people in the coffee shop pretend not to notice. Maybe they think someone we all know has just died. Who knows? And I don't really care. The tears cannot be stopped.

What follows is a narration of most of the transcript of recorded material from that day in the coffee shop. The grammar and vocabulary used are reflecting the translator's knowledge of spoken English at the time of Mo's interview. I have no way of knowing whether the words used are Mo's.

#

I am from ——, small country on Europe-Asia Border. Please do not share exact name of country. My family has no idea where I am. Or even that I live. I do not think many come to Canada from my country, especially gays. I cannot risk identification. If my family locate me, I am dead.

My country has passed nice laws for human rights, but people do not follow when it comes to gays. Things slowly improving for handicapped. It doesn't matter what laws in my country say about discrimination. The law says gays cannot marry but okay for gay sex. But most people don't care about laws. They think it alright to harass gays anyway. I think maybe it worse for trans. People shave hair from girl trans to make them look like boys. Police do nothing to help. Police attack, harm gays and trans. Horrible treatment. Animals slaughtered for meat get more kindness.

I am not religious. I was raised in secular manner, but my family is Muslim, even if they do not worship. If you push, they would probably say gays are offensive for God. Nothing to do with religion, they believe deeply that gay and trans is sickness. Most people in my country, Muslim, Shia, Christian, whatever, think this way.

I never saw gays or even heard about gays where I am born. I grew up in rural area. My family has small farm for local sales. I am one of —— children. All kids work hard on farm before school and at night. My parents say school so important. They want us all to study at university in capital. When one of us graduates, everyone, everyone, is so proud. We are happy family.

I understand from ten or eleven I like boys. I think maybe something is wrong with me. I do not tell my thoughts to people. When I am maybe twelve, thirteen, people talk about parade for gays in big city. Everyone, family, neighbours, all so angry. They say gay is sick, wrong. Men should be with women, the only right way. Anything else is so sick and harmful. They do not want parade here. People say they will kill those in parade.

People in my country so ignorant. Some do not even know about gay. Some say no gays live in my country. Some think trans are same as gay. People think all gay boys are same like girls, all gay girls look like boys. My parents say gays are in big city because of Western influence. None are in farm areas. But I am in farm area. I am gay.

Hearing about the parade, learning about the parade, so wonderful. That, that is first time I learn others are like me. So good. I feel relief. I am not the only one. If there are no gays in my country, so many would not want parade. I see on television many gays. They fight for gay parade.

It is decided there will be no parade for gays in big city. Not anywhere in my country. Parade for gays is banned. Everyone is so happy. But now I know there are so many gays around. We are many. We are so many around the world.

When I am young boy, for sure I cannot say to people I am gay. I cannot get information. I cannot ask. I am so afraid. They will think if you talk about it, maybe you are one. Only information I hear is all gays have sickness of AIDS, all gays rape kids. People think this is true. I know inside me, deep inside, this is not true. I feel so bad. Try so hard to like girls. I like them very much, but not like girlfriends should be. Life is so easy if I like girls. I can make my family proud and happy.

My parents work hard for money to send me to university in capital city. I am very proud and happy to go. The city is way more modern than farm. Possible to have gay relationships if no public touching. Students do not talk much about gays but they know it is there. I hear many say gay not bad and even some countries let gays marry. I go on Internet and learn about rights for gays in other countries. But not in my part of world. For sure not in my country. I am so sad.

At university, many boys wear tight jeans, shirts. I think some are gays. But I don't know how to tell. I meet one boy in class, and I know he is gay. I just know. He tells me he is engaged to marry girl. I am so surprised. Okay. Okay. But later, I learn he does this so nobody knows about the gay. We are now good friends, study and eat together. We talk about gay all the time. I feel so happy. So, so happy. I can finally tell to someone what I hide very deep.

My friend never had sex with girls before, just boys. Girlfriend will wait until they are married for sex. He is so happy. I never had sex with anyone. I ask how he meets boys. He says he meets boys on app. Grindr.

A few times we go to place where gays go. I see gays of many ages and talk to them. They are so nice. I think my family will be angry if they know I go there, but they are not in city. I think they will not find out.

My friend helps me on Grindr. I am so scared but excited. I do not put my true name. I talk to some boys and sometimes meet up to them. I am feeling very okay. I now have friends who are gays. School is okay. I am okay. My family is happy. I study hard.

One day, I agree to meet guy from Grindr. The guy says he goes to university, same like me. My friend comes with me to the meeting place. It is place many gays go, so we are not surprised he picked to meet here. I meet other boys in same place before.

Waiting for the guy, laughing and talking. We are some, few gays from the university together. Many other gays too. Older gays from me and my friend. But then, so much noise. So loud. Confusing. Police race in and arrest people. Everyone is running trying to get out. We are trapped. Most of the guys there get arrested. They treat us bad. Hit and push us hard. Knock us to ground.

Government and police would deny, but they make fake profiles on gays app and then arrest people for torture. Maybe that is what happened. Maybe police were going there to harass gays anyway. I do not know. But we are arrested. Charge is suspicion of gay. There is no law about that, but they arrest us anyway.

My friend is engaged to marry girl, so they release him after few, several hours. I find this information later. We are not together after arrest. They contact his family. I think maybe his family pays them, the police. Having girlfriend is proof for them he is not gay. They are so ignorant. But I am happy my friend safe. He is good, good person.

Police say if I give lots of money, they drop whole thing, but I do not have lots of money. I do not want them to contact my family. They keep me for no reason. I am not the only one. There are many boys here. Locked up. We are so scared.

Very rough and mean police. They take my phone. Then question me about people in my phone, mostly boys. Ask if they, boys, are gays. They ask over and over. No breaks. No food. No water. Nothing. I beg to use the toilet. They watch me pee. When I complain about treatment, they use that as proof of gay. Courage is manly. They think all gays are not like real men. They say I am not a real man. So ignorant.

I only say I know people in phone from university. I tell them I do not know about gays. Two guards say I am lying. They hit me again and again. Over and over. They have wooden sticks. I feel great pain but I do not cry. Tears will be proof of gay.

They keep me four days with awful treatment. There is no crime. No proof of gay. Then, they say they will change the charge to prostitution. Again, no proof. No proof. I am not prostitute. Never. It is against my rights to get this treatment. I say I have rights. They laugh and spit on my face. They hit me many times.

They say I must have medical exam, but it is anal exam. They think they can learn from my bum if I am gay. So ignorant. So cruel. They are so rough. Stretch my bum wide and stick things inside to look. They say I like it. One examines, others watch, laugh. Spit at me.

For the first time, I cry. They laugh more. Call me bad names. Call me girl. Call me names of vagina. Many times, many days they repeat over and over, anal exam. It is worse than beatings.

Also took blood without permissions. I know there are laws against that. I say so. They say prostitutes lose rights. Gays are worse than people who kill and criminals. They do not say why they take blood. I think they will test for sexually transferred disease, but I never found out why. They give me no information.

For six more days they are beating me with wooden sticks, try to force me to sign paper saying I am prostitute. I refuse. I say they have no proof. No right to keep me. I ask for lawyer. They beat me more. Try to force me to sign paper, paper to say I do not want lawyer. But I want lawyer. I do not sign. I demand lawyer. They say no food, no water 'til I sign. Some boys sign. Still I refuse. So no food. Straight guys, prostitutes, criminals, would not be treated this way. No way. Police hate gays.

Then they say they will give electric shock. I am so afraid, but I do not agree to terms. I cannot stand on my legs from beatings. I am weak, tired. Pain like fire all over body. Still, I say nothing. I will die first.

I am lucky. In the end, they do not go through with charges, for prostitute, for gay. For fighting arrest. I get no electric shock. I am so lucky. I find out later many boys get electric shock. Some for many days. Mostly boys who sign paper for no lawyer.

I was there, held, locked for ten days. Horrible. Little food. Little water. No sleep. Repeated anal exam. Hitting over and over with wooden sticks. My body has horrible scars.

I am smart. I know I have rights to keep private my information. I say over and over I have rights. I say do not tell my family, do not contact my family. They have my phone with numbers inside. They do not listen. They call family and say to my father I am arrested for gay sex.

Final charge, disobeying police. So corrupt. Not true. I never fight back when they hit and treat me cruelly. They have no proof for this charge. They say I do not answer about names in my phone. But I know there is no law for this. Finally, they let me go with fine. I have to pay money, maybe like, same like 200 Canadian dollars. Not so much as before.

But now my family, so suspicious. They feel shame from arrest. They ask why I go to areas where gays go. I say it is just place for students for recreation. But they are so angry. The police tell family I confess to gay. This not true. So many lies from police. My family thinks police say truth.

My father says if I am not gay, I can prove it. Just marry. My mother knows nice girls who will marry me. She thinks maybe I am confused. My parents are not religious. I explain before, they are from rural area. They keep old traditions and customs, do not accept gays. My brothers say if I am gay, I am dead. If I have gays for friends, even one, I am still dead.

I cannot agree to marry. If I do, my life over. I might well be dead. And what was beatings for? Anal exams? It is for nothing if I marry girl. I want to live truth.

My family do not take no. Saying no to marry, same as confess to gay. Now they will make sure to protect my family from this awful thing. Gays are poison to family, to country. They think I am dangerous for them and must be killed.

There is no more place for me at home unless I agree to marry. My mother does not speak to me anymore. She tells me I am not her son. No gays in the, her family. She wants me dead. I am so sad. My heart is broke.

I want to stay at university, but my brothers say, say they will come to capital to find me. They will kill me. Police will refuse help. I do not have lots of money. I know, impossible to get job because of arrest. I know. There is no proof of crime, but they will not hire me. People do not hire gays.

Some boys locked with me are fired from jobs, even when no charges or crimes. Police say they are gays. It does not matter if they are true gays. It is what people think. Police say someone gay, they are gay. Whatever police say, true. People do not argue with police. They do not fight for rights of gays. Police do not keep gays safe.

I have no fight. I cannot win. I know, I know from young boy, I am gay. Not confused. Not sick. I will not marry girl.

Some gays from university are hiding. I have nowhere to hide because family against me. I cannot survive without work. Not much money. Situation so hopeless.

I can tell you now about how I got out of country. But please, please, you cannot disclose, things about leaving country in book. People responsible are still there and can help others. I beg of you, for safety. Tell nothing. Say only I left with no suitcase, nothing. School bag stuffed with few things. Not goodbye to anyone. Not even my good friend.

I am just gone.

People who help me find safety say to travel to nearby country. Not require visa for visit. I go where they say. They help with paper. Then, leave with three gays from another country. Other country near mine. Many gays tortured there. True human rights tragedy. They say so many gays in their country kill themselves. So many killed. So many die. I will not die. I am not bad or hurting kids. I am not sick. So much ignorance. We fly to —— and then to Canada. People wait at airport. Bring food and to sleep.

So hard to leave my country. But I leave for life. I will not let police, brothers kill me. In Canada, I must learn new language. I must make new family. Gays my family now.

Just now, few days ago, I meet Russian-Canadian family. They agree to help me so much. They have gay son. That is why. Maybe he can be new brother.

My story is other gay's story. I speak now for those who cannot. Some dead, some hiding. The things you can see on news that happen in Chechnya, in Uganda, happen in my country. And so many other countries. But no media about this. Maybe the world does not know. They cannot care if they do not know. I tell you now, it happens, and true. Tell my story. Please. Maybe someone can care.

Mohammed is common name for boys, Muslim family. When you write book, you can call me Mo.

Update on Mo: the family from Russia with the son who is gay did indeed welcome Mo into their home and they have now become his family. He has had no contact with any members of his biological family since entering Canada as a refugee. He remains petrified that his family will find and kill him. At the time I submitted the book for publication, Mo had just received his work permit and he is seeking employment.

The inspiration for the title of this book came from Mo. He was there, and then he was gone. Completely erased from his country and his life.

#

Mo requested that his birth country remain anonymous. And the exact country where he is from doesn't matter because it isn't the point. He could have been born in any number of countries bordering or near Russia that do not provide human rights or protections for people with unconventional sexual orientations or gender identity or expression.

Back in 2017, the news was inundated with stories about the treatment of homosexual men in the Chechnya Republic, part of the Russian Federation.[33] This country was accused of rounding up men believed to be gay, placing them in custodial camps, and torturing them. Reports of public humiliation and brutalization of homosexual men were extensive. Chechen police are still known to pose as being gay to lure homosexual men into meeting them. They subsequently assault their prey, and then steal their phone contacts to add to the list of suspected homosexuals, irrespective of whether or not these people are homosexual. The intent of these atrocities seems to be a cleansing of the country of anything homosexual, or anything viewed as gender non-conforming.

While multiple other sources confirmed that these stories and reports are true, Ramzan Kadyrov, head of the Chechen Republic, denied these allegations on the grounds that there were no gay people in Chechnya, or anywhere in Russia.[34] He also reported that even if such people existed, which he doubted, their families would have already taken care of the problem.

These anti-gay crusades continue today as Russia is guilty of multiple human rights violations, not only those against 2SLGBTQ+ people. Hate crimes because of sexuality or gender identity are not investigated in Russia so it is difficult to extract accurate information as to what is occurring. Since Russia invaded Ukraine in February 2022, there has been an even harsher crackdown on independent journalism, as well as the deliberate silencing of any public criticism or expression of anything outside of what the government condones. It is known that there have been bills passed so that information not supporting Putin's perspective on what is occurring in the country cannot be disseminated.[35] At the same time, Russia has not lightened up on their attack of 2SLGBTQ+ people. According to the 2023 Human Rights Watch World Report,[36] Russia has proposed new homophobic legislation and forced the closure of the largest human rights organization there. Unfortunately, men remaining in their homeland who manage to survive brutalities against them because of their sexuality are then outed to their families, who are encouraged to perform whatever punishments might be necessary. Refugees from that part of the world have indicated that even if the government denies it, they have hinted very strongly to the people that killing gay people be perfectly acceptable, and even desirable. Some men escaping execution are now in extreme danger, as they are being hunted like animals by their own families. Many lives in Russia are currently in grave danger, and the situation for people who are 2SLGBTQ+ remains grim.

Chechnya, like Russia, has continued its overt attacks on people who identify as 2SLGBTQ+ as well as their allies. Some Chechen refugees who are gay, primarily men, have been brought secretly from Russia into Canada to protect them from these brutalities. The details of how this happens are not publicized or discussed. This parallels Mo's experience somewhat, because the manner which he was brought out of his country and any organizations that facilitated his getaway have been kept confidential.

Mo's account of surviving flagrant cruelty, including repeated anal examinations by so-called law-enforcers to determine his sexuality, is not limited to his home country. Other countries elsewhere in the world reported to share this same deplorable practice include Cameroon, Egypt, Kenya, Lebanon, Saudi Arabia, Sri Lanka, Tunisia, Turkmenistan, United Arab Emirates, Uganda, Uzbekistan, and Zambia, although these reports are difficult to confirm. There is absolutely no justification for this occurrence.[37] Anal examinations on men for the purpose of identifying their sexual orientation are a form of torture, a blatant act of degradation, and a complete violation of human rights.[37]

Closing Thoughts

The conditions 2SLGBTQ+ people endure around the world are not just 2SLGBTQ+ concerns, and this is not about the propagation of some mythical, liberal, gay agenda that seeks to undermine people's religious beliefs and the structure of the conventional family. 2SLGBTQ+ rights are human rights. And if you happen to be someone who doesn't care about people who are 2SLGBTQ+, or even has disdain for us and wishes we would all just put our rainbow flags away, then please consider that human rights denied to 2SLGBTQ+ people, or Indigenous people, or any other oppressed group for that matter, are fundamentally yours to lose. If we can be denied our human rights, it might not be too much of a stretch for you to be denied yours.

This fight is for all of us. We need to stop pretending that the world is a safe place for 2SLGBTQ+ people. And we need to stop fooling ourselves into believing that 2SLGBTQ+ rights are not in any way related to the global oppression of women and gender-based violence, because they are intimately linked. It is deeply offensive and condescending to think otherwise.

Human rights are just that, rights for all humans. They are not just for people who hold the same political views as you and choose to worship the way that you do. They are not just for people who share your ethnicity and speak familiar languages, and not just for people with a specific colour of skin pigmentation. By their very definition, human rights are not for one specific gender or sexual orientation. And they are not a privilege. They are for everyone.

The plight of 2SLGBTQ+ people globally challenges our humanitarian beliefs at our very core. Until we recognize and acknowledge the cruelties that have occurred and continue to occur against 2SLGBTQ+ people around the world, we have no chance of affecting any real change. We need to become accountable for these atrocities.

This means acknowledging stories in their totality; even when it is uncomfortable to learn about them, even when the events that occur make us physically ill and keep us awake at night. It is time for everyone to step up and face what occurs when we ignore the hate and continue to permit homophobia and transphobia to continue. It is time to acknowledge the pain our complicity allows.

Please do not get lulled into complacency about the state of human rights and the treatment of people who are 2SLGBTQ+ in Canada or globally because you happen to notice more gay characters on television, you have a gay friend, and you have attended a drag show or two. Maybe you have even watched a Pride parade. Don't get fooled. Things are not okay, it is never easy, and in many places, it is lethal to identify as being 2SLGBTQ+.

While running around the streets waving rainbow flags during Pride month might signal some sense of broader acceptance for 2SLGBTQ+ people, I believe that an emphasis on the over-consumption of alcoholic beverages, partying, and consumerism diverts attention away from the grotesque human rights violations against 2SLGBTQ+ people that are occurring globally, every day.

I am not suggesting that people shouldn't enjoy Pride activities. We have every right to celebrate our existence, acknowledge how far we have come, continue to demand humane and unbiased treatment, and to occupy space without fear or apology. What I am saying is that we also need to continue to raise awareness of the grim realities of 2SLGBTQ+ people around the world who battle unsafe, inhumane living conditions and indescribable, brutal violence. Many are so marginalized they die on the streets, many are murdered, or commit suicide.

In less aggressively homophobic and transphobic countries, there continue to be inequities in health care, policing, the penal system, and other services, even when the country is considered "safe and welcoming." The message needs to get out there that the status quo is *not okay*. This is about securing and maintaining basic human rights.

What's more, allowing 2SLGBTQ+ refugees into our country shouldn't just be something on someone's political checklist. Landing here is only the beginning. They need a tremendous amount of support in transitioning to life here. That doesn't just mean government assistance with housing, food, and finding employment, or provision of programs for learning a new language. It includes kindness, respect, and support from all of us.

I have a deep, moral obligation to the people I interviewed to tell their stories as authentically as I can and to the best of my ability. They have the right to have their experiences acknowledged and to be recognized by all of us who are culpable for the cruelties they have endured.

I want to encourage all people who came to Canada as refugees because they were unsafe in their countries due to their sexual orientation or gender identity or expression to continue to tell and retell their stories. It will take time for people to process them. Eventually, more people will become educated, more will have their eyes and their minds opened. Listening to these stories and writing a book about them does not make me an expert. Far from it. I am only just beginning to comprehend what people who identify as being 2SLGBTQ+ endure around the world. People just like me. I am one of the lucky ones. I happened to be born in a country where I am guaranteed my human rights. Writing this book has forced me to question myself as a queer woman: do I fight for the rights of other 2SLGBTQ+ people who do not own my privilege?

The people who I interviewed represent only themselves and their own personal journeys. They represent just a handful of countries. Every single one of them is unique in the atrocities they have endured and the barriers they have encountered along the way. However, they do share one thing in common. They believed they could be freed. They clung to a glimmer of hope, and to their personhood, and they survived. I remain humbled by their courage.

My take on their collective message is that they want the (privileged) world to become aware of the atrocities that they, and so many others, bore because of their sexual orientation or gender identity or expression. They want it to stop. And they want the hate to be gone.

As Mo explicitly stated:

Maybe the world does not know. They cannot care if they do not know. I tell you now, it happens, and is true. Tell my story. Please. Maybe someone can care.

Maybe.

Acknowledgments

I would like to express my heartfelt gratitude to the people who I interviewed for this book, whose courage is beyond measure. Their trust in me was and continues to be overwhelming. They all need to know that meeting them has forever changed me in ways that transcend any words I could write. It would be impossible to explain the depth of what the experience of meeting them has meant. So, I won't try. All I can say is thank you.

I would like to thank my wife, my adult children, and my family, both biological and chosen, for giving me the time and space to process the horrific atrocities most of these people have endured. Hearing these stories forced me to confront the darkest and most vile side of human beings. I couldn't have completed this work if I did not feel so completely safe and loved.

Finally, I would like to acknowledge Rebecca Eckler, Chloe Robinson, Sasha Stoltz, and everyone on the RE:BOOKS publishing team for their hard work in making this book real. To Deanna McFadden, thank you for recognizing how emotionally difficult it was to put the personal journeys people shared with me into words.

REFERENCES

Introduction

1. Choi, A., & Razo, J. (2024, February 16). *Where Same-Sex Marriage Is Legal around the World*. CNN. Retrieved March 11, 2024, from https://www.cnn.com/world/same-sex-marriage-legal-countries-map-dg/index.html

2. UNHCR (n.d.). *Global Population Planning Figures 2024*. UNHCR Global Appeal 2024. Retrieved March 11, 2024, from https://reporting.unhcr.org/global-appeal-2024-6383

3. The Trevor Project (2021, December 15). *Facts about Suicide among LGBTQ+ Young People*. The Trevor Project LGBTQ+ Resources. Retrieved October 3, 2023, from https://www.thetrevorproject.org/resources/article/facts-about-lgbtq-youth-suicide/

4. World Health Organization (2024, February 5). *Female Genital Mutilation*. Retrieved March 11, 2024, from https://www.who.int/news-room/fact-sheets/detail/female-genital-mutilation

5. Hoskin, R.A., Blair, K.L., & Holmberg, D. (2024). Femmephobia Is a Uniquely Powerful Predictor of Anti-Gay Behavior. *Archives of Sexual Behavior, 53*(1), 127–140.

6. Global Citizen (2022, November 8). *Trans Murder Monitoring*. Transrespect versus Transphobia Worldwide. Retrieved January 23, 2023, from https://transrespect.org/en/research/tmm/

7. Human Rights Watch (2022). World Report 2022, events of 2021. (pp. 711, 721–722). https://www.hrw.org/sites/default/files/media_2022/01/World%20Report%202022%20web%20pdf_0.pdf

8. Human Rights Watch (2023). World Report 2023, events of 2022. (p. 673). https://www.hrw.org/sites/default/files/media_2023/01/World_Report_2023_WE BSPREADS_0.pdf

References

9. Jones, D., & Franklin J. (2022). *Not Just Florida. More than a Dozen States Propose So-Called "Don't Say Gay" Bills*. National Public Radio (NPR) Politics. Retrieved January 5, 2024 from https://www.npr.org/2022/04/10/1091543359/15-states-dont-say-gay-anti-transgender-bills

10. Government of Canada (n.d.). *Police Reported Hate Crime 2021*. Statistics Canada. Retrieved July 11, 2023, from https://www150.statcan.gc.ca/n1/daily-quotidien/230322/dq230322a-eng.htm

11. Immigration and Refugee Board of Canada (2023, October 31). *Chairperson's Guideline 4: Gender Considerations in Proceedings before the Immigration and Refugee Board*. Retrieved January 5, 2024, from https://www.irb-cisr.gc.ca/en/legal-policy/policies/Pages/GuideDir04.aspx

Sherwin's Story

12. Allyn, Angela R. (2012). Homophobia in Jamaica: A Study of Cultural Heterosexism in Praxis. *Social Science Research Network*, 1–45.

13. Padgett, T. (2006, April 6). *The Most Homophobic Place on Earth?* Time. Retrieved March 16, 2021, from https://content.time.com/time/world/article/0,8599,1182991,00.html

14. Ghoshal, N. (2021, February 17). *Human Rights Body Calls for Repeal of Jamaica's Anti-LGBT Laws*. Human Rights Watch. Retrieved July 20, 2023, from https://www.hrw.org/news/2021/02/17/human-rights-body-calls-repeal-jamaicas-anti-lgbt-laws

Sungai's Story

15. (n.d.). *Exorcism*. United States Conference of Catholic Bishops. Retrieved March 17, 2024, from https://www.usccb.org/prayer-and-worship/sacraments-and-sacramentals/sacramentals-blessings/exorcism

16. United Nations (n.d.). *Convention against Torture and Other Cruel, Inhumane or Degrading Treatment or Punishment*. United Nations Human Rights Office of the High Commission. Retrieved March

17, 2024, from https://www.ohchr.org/en/instruments-mechanisms/
instruments/convention-against-torture-and-other-cruel-inhuman-or-
degrading

17. Fitzsimons, T. (2020, June 13). *U.N. Calls for Global End to Conversion Therapy, Says It "May Amount to Torture."* NBC News. Retrieved March 7, 2024, from https://www.nbcnews.com/feature/nbc-out/u-n-calls-global-end-conversion-therapy-says-it-may-n1230851

18. Human Rights Watch (2022, December 8). *Indonesia: New Criminal Code Disastrous for Rights.* Human Rights Watch. Retrieved January 9, 2023, from https://www.hrw.org/news/2022/12/08/indonesia-new-criminal-code-disastrous-rights

Ariella's Story

19. Raines, J. (2023). *The T in LGBT: Everything You Need to Know about Being Trans.* Kindle Edition. Ebury Digital (June 29, 2023). Available in hardcover May 24, 2024.

20. Solomon, E. (2023). Nigeria's Same Sex Marriage Prohibition Act: Flying in the Faces of Constitutional and African Charter Rights. *Nigerian Bar Journal, 13*(2), 141–169.

21. International Organization for Migration (IOM) (2022, June 13). *Nigeria North-East Displacement Report 41.* IOM Displacement Tracking Matrix. Retrieved January 23, 2023, from https://dtm.iom.int/reports/nigeria-north-east-displacement-report-41-june-2022.

22. Human Rights Watch (2022). World Report 2022, events of 2021. (p. 499). https://www.hrw.org/sites/default/files/media_2022/01/World%20Report%202022%20web%20pdf_0.pdf

23. BBC News (2023, March 31). *Homosexuality: The Countries Where It Is Illegal to Be Gay.* Retrieved March 7, 2024, from https://www.bbc.com/news/world-43822234

24. Rakhetsi, A. (2021, February 25). *6 Countries in Africa That Have Legalized Same-Sex Relationships in the Past 10 Years.* Global Citizen News. Retrieved January 23, 2023, from https://www.globalcitizen.org/en/content/countries-legalized-same-sex-relationships-africa/

25. Human Rights Campaign (2022, November 8). *Fatal Violence against the Transgender and Gender-Expansive Community in 2022*. Human Rights Campaign Resources. Retrieved January 23, 2023, from https://www.hrc.org/resources/fatal-violence-against-the-transgender-and-gender-expansive-community-in-2022

Ziad and Mazn's Story

26. UNHCR The UN Refugee Agency (n.d.). *The 1951 Refugee Convention*. UNHCR Global Website. Retrieved January 8, 2024, from https://www.unhcr.org/about-unhcr/who-we-are/1951-refugee-convention

27. (2024, March 14). *Syrian Refugee Crisis Explained*. USA for UNHCR. The UN Refugee Agency. Retrieved March 14, 2024, from https://www.unrefugees.org/news/syria-refugee-crisis-explained/

Roberto and Eric's Story

28. DeLuzio, J. (2021). *Surviving the Closet. Learning to Live after Coming Out Later in Life*. RE:BOOKS Publishing.

29. Human Rights Watch (2022). World Report 2022, events of 2021. (pp. 449–460). https://www.hrw.org/sites/default/files/media_2022/01/World%20Report%202022%20web%20pdf_0.pdf

30. Human Rights Watch (2023). World Report 2023, events of 2022. (pp. 411–419). https://www.hrw.org/sites/default/files/media_2023/01/World_Report_2023_WEBSPREADS_0.pdf

Maryam's Story

31. United States Commission on International Religious Freedom (USCIRF) (2023). *Shari'a and LGBTI Persons. The Use of Shari'a as Religious Justification for Capital Punishment against LGBTI Persons [Fact Sheet]*. https://www.uscirf.gov/sites/default/files/2021-03/2021%20Factsheet%20-%20Sharia%20and%20LGBTI.pdf

32. Pirnia, B., & Pirnia, K. (2022). Sex Reassignment Surgery in Iran, Rebirth or Human Rights Violations against Transgender People? *Iranian Journal of Public Health*, *51*(11), 2632–2633.

Mo's Story

33. Human Rights Watch (2017, May 26). *"They Have Long Arms and They Can Find Me." Anti-Gay Purge by Local Authorities in Russia's Chechen Republic*. Retrieved March 7, 2024, from https://www.hrw.org/report/2017/05/26/they-have-long-arms-and-they-can-find-me/anti-gay-purge-local-authorities-russias

34. Walker, S. (2017, April 21). *Chechnya Leader Rejects Reports of Anti-gay Purge*. Retrieved March 7, 2024, from https://www.theguardian.com/world/2017/apr/21/chechnya-leader-rejects-reports-of-anti-gay-purge

35. Human Rights Watch (2022, April 7). *Russia Criminalizes Independent War Reporting, Anti-War Protests*. Retrieved March 7, 2024, from https://www.hrw.org/news/2022/03/07/russia-criminalizes-independent-war-reporting-anti-war-protests

36. Human Rights Watch (2023). World Report 2023, events of 2022. (pp. 505 & 506).

37. Cichowitz C., Rubenstein L., & Beyrer C. (2018). Forced Anal Examinations to Ascertain Sexual Orientation and Sexual Behavior: An Abusive and Medically Unsound Practice. *PLoS Med, 15*(3). doi: 10.1371/journal.pmed.1002536.

How You Can Help

1. Find out what organizations provide support and assistance to 2SLGBTQ+ refugees in your area, for example, Rainbow Railroad (www.rainbowroad.org), a global not-for-profit organization based in the United States and Canada that helps at-risk 2SLGBTQ+ people get to safety worldwide. Donate money if you are able, or volunteer your time if they are seeking volunteers.

References

2. Financially sponsor a 2SLGBTQ+ refugee. Check your federal government website for information on the process where you live. In Canada, this will be available on the Government of Canada website.

3. Private sponsorship may be available in your area. Check with your federal authorities.

4. Provide temporary housing for new 2SLGBTQ+ refugees in your home. It is also possible to rent a room in your home to a refugee who is beginning their resettlement process. There will be local resources where you live to provide information on this.

5. Hire a 2SLGBTQ+ refugee who has a work permit.

6. Donate money to organizations providing health services to refugees, particularly for those people living with HIV/AIDS. Many people who are 2SLGBTQ+ refugees were unable to access health services in their home countries.

7. Become informed and be an advocate. Keep yourself current on what is occurring globally around the world to people who are 2SLGBTQ+, and then provide information to your friends and colleagues.

8. Examine your own biases and attitudes about people who identify as 2SLGBTQ+. You don't have to approve of their identity to agree that their rights are human rights, and they are entitled to protection under the law.

9. Challenge people when they make homophobic or transphobic jokes or comments, when you feel safe to do so. Attitudes and biases are slow to change and language matters.

10. Do not vote for politicians who seek to deny people who identify as 2SLGBTQ+ basic human rights and protections. Endorse and vote for candidates who do support 2SLGBTQ+ rights and refugees.

TERMINOLOGY

Asexual (Ace): A person who experiences little or no sexual attraction and/or desire for sexual contact and/or interest in participating in sexual relationships. They may or may not have romantic feelings or interest in romantic relationships. People who are ace are diverse in their identities.

Aromantic (Aro): A person who experiences little or no romantic attraction or interest in engaging in romantic relationships. People who are aromantic are diverse in their identities. They may or may not also be Ace.

Biological sex: A classification based on genitals, hormones, and chromosomes. The sex a person is assigned at birth is usually designated by the appearance of their external genitalia.

Bisexual: A person who is attracted to or interested in forming intimate relationships with someone of a different gender. There is variation in how people who identify as bisexual define what a man is and what a woman is, and people who are bisexual may not only be attracted to binary genders.

Cisgender: A person whose gender matches the gender they were assigned at birth.

Cishet: A cishet person is cisgender and heterosexual.

Closeted, living in the closet: Someone who is aware they have a non-conventional sexual orientation or gender identity but does not tell anyone.

Coming out; coming out of the closet: The process of telling people in some or all your life networks that you have a non-conventional sexual orientation, gender identity, or gender expression. This is often an on-going process.

Femmephobia: Dislike or hostility towards women and or people who present in a feminine manner. The devaluing of anything feminine or associated with femininity.

Terminology

Gay: A term used to refer to people with same-gender attraction or interest in pursuing intimate relationships with people of the same gender. It is more often used to refer to men who experience same-gender attraction.

Gender: A person's feelings or identity of being a man, a woman, both, neither, or something else.

Gender binary: The classification of gender as being either male or female.

Gender-based violence: Abuse and harm against women, girls, and trans feminine people, which is tied to the systemic power difference between men and women.

Heterosexual—commonly referred to as "straight": A person who experiences attraction or interest in pursuing intimate relationships with people of a different gender. The term "heterosexuality" is often defined as people who desire men–women coupling. However, people who are intersex or transgender can also identify as straight.

Homophobia: A broad term referring to a wide range of negative feelings, attitudes, and actions, including violent and oppressive actions and behaviours, towards people who identify or are perceived as homosexual. It may or may not be based on fear.

Homosexual: An older word that refers to a person who experiences attraction or interest in pursuing intimate relationships with people of the same gender (i.e., gay or lesbian). This word is often seen as offensive today because it was and still is sometimes used as a medical term that views people with a non-conventional sexual orientation as suffering from a disorder of behaviour.

Intersex: An umbrella term used to describe people who carry variations in their reproductive and/or sexual anatomy that differ from what is traditionally considered male or female. People who are intersex were historically called hermaphrodites, but that term is no longer used for humans and is considered derogatory.

Lesbian: Women who experience exclusively or primarily same-gender attraction or interest in pursuing intimate relationships with other women.

LGBTQQIP2SA+ (LGBTQ2S+ for short): An acronym that stands for Lesbian, Gay, Bisexual, Transgender, Queer, Questioning, Intersex, Pansexual, Two-spirit, Asexual. There are other versions of this acronym.

Historically, the A was used to stand for Ally, but it is now more commonly used to encompass Asexual, Aromantic, and Agender.

Non-binary gender: An umbrella term for gender identities that do not fit into a male-female dichotomy.

Pansexual: A person who is attracted to or interested in forming intimate relationships with people regardless of gender identity.

Queer: An umbrella term that is sometimes used to refer to any person with a non-conventional sexual orientation and/or gender identity. This is not a universally accepted term. Some people find it offensive.

Questioning: Refers to the state of questioning one's sexual orientation and/or gender identity.

Transgender or trans: An umbrella term for people whose gender identity is different from the gender they were assigned at birth. This includes trans women who were initially labelled as boys, trans men who were initially labelled as girls, and a range of non-binary people who feel their gender does not fit into the gender binary, as well as gender non-conforming people.

Transphobia: A broad term referring to a wide range of negative feelings, attitudes, and actions, including violent and oppressive actions and behaviours, towards people who identify or are perceived as transgender or gender non-conforming. It may or may not be based on fear.

Two-spirit: An umbrella term used within some Indigenous communities that designates having both a masculine and a feminine spirit. It encompasses cultural, spiritual, sexual, and gender identities within Indigenous communities. A person might identify as two-spirit for a variety of gender and/or sexual identity reasons.

THEMES AND TOPICS FOR DISCUSSION

1. Was there one interview that you found the most difficult?
2. What changes would you like to see globally for people who identify as being 2SLGBTQ+ that might make the world safer for them?
3. What do you think are common misconceptions about people who are seeking asylum because of their sexual orientation or gender identity?
4. Are you aware of the laws around human rights and protection of people who are gay, transgender, or gender non-conforming where you live and what the repercussions are for breaking these laws? If there are laws, are they upheld?
5. Before you read this book, were you aware of the treatment of people who are gay, transgender, or gender non-conforming globally? Will you do anything differently now that you have read it?
6. How has the increased presence of 2SLGBTQ+ people in television shows, movies, and other media in some parts of the world helped or worsened the acceptance of people who are gay, transgender, or gender non-conforming?
7. The author presents the perspective that much of the bullying and violence directed at people who are gay, transgender, or gender non-conforming globally is linked to the oppression of women and gender-based violence. What do you think or feel about this?
8. How do the socially accepted gender roles for men and women that continue to be prominent impact people who are both heterosexual and cisgender?